MAKING LIFE MEANINGFUL

May whoever sees, touches, reads, remembers, or talks or thinks about these publications never be reborn in unfortunate circumstances, receive only rebirths in situations conducive to the perfect practice of Dharma, meet only perfectly qualified spiritual guides, quickly develop bodhicitta and immediately attain enlightenment for the sake of all sentient beings.

Lama Zopa Rinpoche

Making Life Meaningful

Edited by Nicholas Ribush

Lama Yeshe Wisdom Archive • Boston

www.LamaYeshe.com
A non-profit charitable organization for the benefit of all
sentient beings and a section of the Foundation for the
Preservation of the Mahayana Tradition
www.fpmt.org

First published 2001
15,000 copies for free distribution

LAMA YESHE WISDOM ARCHIVE
PO BOX 356
WESTON
MA 02493 USA

ISBN 1-891868-07-1

10 9 8 7 6 5 4 3 2 1

Cover photographs by Ven. Roger Kunsang
Cover design by Carol Maglitta
Book design by Mark Gatter
Printed in Canada on recycled, acid-free paper

Please contact the LAMA YESHE WISDOM ARCHIVE for copies of
our free booklets

CONTENTS

BENEFACTOR'S DEDICATION

In loving memory of my dear parents Glenice and Jack Custy, who were renowned among their friends and associates for their kindness, integrity and wisdom; who gave me a perfect human rebirth with the best education and enjoyments; and who showed me through their example as parents the meaning of self-sacrifice, honesty and unconditional love. In all their future lives, may they only have good health, happiness and ease in most quickly perfecting the path to Enlightenment.

Through the clear flawless teachings of my precious spiritual parents Lama Yeshe and Lama Zopa Rinpoche, I have a little understanding of the meaning of mother and father sentient beings' incredible kindness and suffering. May Lama Ösel Rinpoche and Lama Zopa Rinpoche live long healthy lives and all their wishes be fulfilled without hindrance.

—Ecie Hursthouse

PUBLISHER'S ACKNOWLEDGMENTS

We are extremely grateful to our friends and supporters who have made it possible for the LAMA YESHE WISDOM ARCHIVE to both exist and function: to Lama Yeshe and Lama Zopa Rinpoche, whose kindness is impossible to repay; to Peter and Nicole Kedge and Venerable Ailsa Cameron for helping bring the ARCHIVE to its present state of development; to Venerable Roger Kunsang, Lama Zopa's tireless assistant, for his kindness and consideration; and to our sustaining supporters: Drs. Penny Noyce & Leo Liu, Barry & Connie Hershey, Joan Terry, Roger & Claire Ash-Wheeler, Claire Atkins, Ecie Hursthouse, Lily Chang Wu, T. Y. Alexander, Therese Miller, Chris Dornan, Henry & Catherine Lau, Tom & Suzanne Castles, Datuk Tai Tsu Kuang, Chuah Kok Leng, the Caytons (Lori, Karuna, Pam, Bob & Amy), Tom Thorning, Tan Swee Eng, Salim Lee, Doren & Mary Harper, Claire Ritter, Sandra Magnussen, Cecily Drucker, Lynnea Elkind, Janet Moore, Su Hung, Carol Davies, Jack Morison, Dorian Ribush and Dharmawati Brechbuhl. We also thank most sincerely Massimo Corona and the FPMT International Office for their generous financial and administrative assistance.

We are especially grateful to Ecie Hursthouse for sponsoring the editorial preparation of this book in memory of her late parents, for their sake and for that of all sentient beings.

Lama Zopa Rinpoche has said that sponsoring the publication of Dharma teachings in memory of deceased relatives and friends was very common in Tibet and is of great benefit. Therefore, the LAMA YESHE WISDOM ARCHIVE encourages others who might like to make booklets of teachings by Lama Yeshe and Lama Zopa Rinpoche available for free distribution in this way to contact us for more information. Thank you so much.

We would also like to acknowledge the great kindness of Richard Gere and the Gere Foundation for so compassionately supporting the ARCHIVE since its inception and for making a generous grant to help cover the printing of this book, and to thank Jennifer Greenfield for her kind assistance over these many years.

We thank our friends in Hong Kong for also helping with the publication of this book: Ven. Pemba, Francis Siu, Khado, Alvin Leong, Twinkie Leung, Katie Chan and Esther Ngai.

We would like, as well, to express our appreciation for the kindness and compassion of all those generous benefactors who have contributed to the ARCHIVE since our last publication, *The Essence of Tibetan Buddhism*. Therefore, for donations received between February and May, 2001, we extend a huge thank you to Judy B. Adams, Ven. Bob Alcorn, Jan Victoria Angel, Leticia Anson, Rako Araki, Christine Arlington, Yong Meng Beh, Peggy Bennington, Avi Bonfil, Donald Bonney, Melanie Bryan, Buddha Maitreya Study Group, Sharon Cardamone, John Carmody, Kendra Carpenter, Chang Jin Meng & family, Chew Min Chuan, Michael Childs, Larry Chiriboga, Neil Christopherson, Chung Kim Chuan, Maggie Claydon, John Edward Custy III, MaryAnn Czermak, Jonathan Danziger, John Deluca, Jhamba Dolkar, Richard Donnelly, Herbert J. Dorris, Jan Eldridge, Sarah Feifel, Ven. Damchö Finnegan, Dionne Fomby, Krishna Kanta Ghosh, Ken Goddard, Stanley Goldberg, Carleen Gonder, Bob Gottlieb, Alnis Grants & Aryatara Institute, Holly June Graves, Laura Guerreiro-Ramos, James Hagan, Judith A. Hardenburg, Richard Hay, Lella Heins, Silke Heleine, Myron Helmer, Bosco Ho, Sandra Howell, T.Y. Hsieh, Roger Jackson, James W. Johns, Gay Judson, Bill Kelley & Robyn Brentano, Toni Kenyon, Allan W. King, Camille Kozlowski, Dieter Kratzer, Jasmine Krotkov, Lorne & Terry Ladner, Chiu-Mei Lai & Anthony Stowe, Willem Langelaan, Melanie Law, Harry Leong, John Liberty, Loh Seng, Ky Truong Ly, Janusz Madej, Ingrid J. Magdahl, Fred Martinson, Phil McDonald, Robert McDonough, Ellen McInerny, S. McKelvey, Hope McLeod, John McMann, Sybil Miller, Carol Moss, Ven. Thubten Munsel, Robert Mueller, Michael Myers, Wanda Nettl, John & Beth Newman, Giang Nguyen, Kimchung Nguyen, Emi Okuda, Janet Olsen, Jeri Opalk, Gregory & Anna Osborne, Chris Overall, Pek See Ah Peng, James Pelkey, Robert Phipps, Michele Picozzi Paterson, Giovanna Pescetti, George Propps, Karen Rice, Wendy Ridley, Rev. Janyce Riedel, P. Rind, Tamara Salmutter, Jesse Sartain, Angie Sassano, K.B. Schaetzel-Hill, Douglas Schamerhorn, Alexandria Schiller, James Schmitt,

Amy Sedivy, Deanna Sheriff, Beth Lee Simon, Ed Softky, Khuslen Soninbayar, Jack Sonnabaum & Judith Hunt, Robert Soto, Sheridan Sperry, Gareth Sparham, Margaret Spoor, Jennifer Sprowl, Lana Sundberg, Vincenzo Tallarico, Janet Tan, Sandra Tatlock, Thubten Norbu Ling, Sandra & Sander Tideman, Wilhelmina van de Poll, Lerie Alstad von Ells, Robbie Watkins, Susan Webster, Kate Lila Wheeler, Joseph Williams, Jan Willis, Carol Arredondo Wolovsky and Murray Wright.

Great thanks are also due to the following Australian supporters who contributed through our Melbourne office and have not been specifically thanked before: Will & Lyndy Abram, Roger Amos, Atisha Centre, Nella Binnendijk, Norma Brahatis, Buddhist Library Meditation Centre, Ven. Losang Chodron, Gerda Cohen, Christine Conlon, Ven. Thubten Dolma, Brian Dwyer, Frances Kelly, Langri Tangpa Centre, Yvonne Malykke, Shirley Marshall, Carolyn McLeod, Pauline McLoughlin, Debby Mientjes, Nancy Patton, David Roberts, Zarna & Anil Somaia, Ken Somers, Adam Struzynski, Vajrasattva Mountain Centre, Diana van Die, Theo van Embden and Ingrid Vickery-Howe.

Finally, we would also like to thank the many kind people who have asked that their donations be kept anonymous; the volunteers who have given so generously of their time to help us with our mailings; Alison Ribush & Mandala Books (Melbourne) for much appreciated assistance with our work in Australia; and Dennis Heslop, Philip Bradley and our other friends at Wisdom Books (London) for their great help with our work in Europe.

If you, dear reader, would like to join this noble group of open-hearted altruists by contributing to the production of more free booklets by Lama Yeshe or Lama Zopa Rinpoche or to any other aspect of the LAMA YESHE WISDOM ARCHIVE's work, please contact us to find out how.

Through the merit of having contributed to the spread of the Buddha's teachings for the sake of all sentient beings, may our benefactors and their families and friends have long and healthy lives, all happiness, and may all their Dharma wishes be instantly fulfilled.

Editor's Introduction

In this book, Lama Zopa Rinpoche explains how we can practice Dharma, the true cause of happiness, twenty-four hours a day. For most of us, it is extremely important to know how to do this. Our busy lives do not allow us the luxury of many hours' formal study and practice each day. We have to work, eat, sleep, fulfill family and societal obligations, entertain ourselves and so forth—activities that are not normally considered to be spiritual pursuits. Who has time to meditate?

However, as Rinpoche points out again and again, Dharma is not just what you do but the way that you do it. Motivation is key. It's our mental attitude and not so much the action itself that determines whether what we do is positive, the cause of happiness, or negative, the cause of suffering. Therefore, if we know how to use our mind properly, everything we do can become a Dharma action, good karma, meritorious, positive. In these teachings, then, Rinpoche clarifies how we should use our minds so that we can make everything we do the true cause of happiness.

But that's not all. There are different degrees of happiness, the highest being that of enlightenment; buddhahood itself. That is what we must strive for, but not for ourselves alone. We must aim for the enlightenment of all sentient beings; we must endeavor to bring the highest degree of happiness to every single living being. To work with compassion for the enlightenment of all sentient beings is the purpose of our lives, and to direct everything we do towards this goal is how we can make our lives as meaningful as they can possibly be.

Such motivation is called bodhicitta, and in this book, Lama Zopa Rinpoche describes how we can motivate our every action with bodhicitta, the true cause of ultimate happiness for all sentient beings. To live by bodhicitta is to live a truly meaningful life. Thank you, Rinpoche, for your never-ending kindness in being a perfect example of bodhicitta in action and for constantly teaching us the importance of this. May you live long for the benefit of all sentient beings.

The first talk, "The Purpose of Life," was given in New York City, August, 1999, at the request of Geshe Michael Roach, during a three-day series of teachings by His Holiness the Dalai Lama. The other teachings in this booklet form the essence of a full-length book in preparation, which will explain in more detail how to make our daily lives meaningful and will contain details of specific practices that Rinpoche recommends we do. These include making light offerings, liberating animals and offering water to Dzambhala and the pretas, current versions of which may be found in Rinpoche's recently published book, *Teachings from the Vajrasattva Retreat.*

I would like to thank Su Hung and Wendy Cook for their help with the New York talk, many other people, including Vens. Yeshe Khadro, Ailsa Cameron and Connie Miller and Linda Gatter for their help with the other material, as well as Mark Gatter and Carol Maglitta for designing this book.

ONE

THE PURPOSE OF LIFE

COMPASSION

For those of us who have been able to attend His Holiness the Dalai Lama's teachings on Kamalashila's *Gom-rim* these past few days, this is a most precious, unbelievably fortunate time. It is just incredible that we have the karma to be able to see the Buddha of Compassion in human form. Thus, not only can we communicate with this living manifestation of the enlightened mind but we can also receive teachings on a path that without doubt, without any question, liberates us from both the ocean of samsaric suffering and its cause—karma, which are actions motivated by delusion, and the delusions themselves, the disturbing, obscuring thoughts whose continuity has no beginning. Even if we cannot practice every single thing that His Holiness has taught these past few days, just hearing his teachings leaves positive imprints on our mental continua, and sooner or later, these imprints will definitely liberate us from the ocean of samsaric suffering and its cause and bring us to full enlightenment, the peerless happiness of buddhahood.

In these teachings, His Holiness has been talking about compassion. What is the purpose of our lives? Why do we live?

Why do we exert so much effort to survive every day, every hour, every minute, every second? Why do we spend so much money taking care of this body, checking our health every year to see if there's anything wrong and, if there is, undergoing expensive treatment? Why do we spend so much money on food, clothing and shelter—on the many things we need to survive and be healthy? Why do we do all those billions of exercises to keep our bodies healthy?

All these expenses and activities have meaning only if we have compassion within us. Compassion for others makes everything we do—spending money, studying, working, exercizing, looking after our health—meaningful.

If, on the other hand, our hearts lack compassion, our lives become empty. All those expenses, all that effort, all those long hours on the job are totally devoid of meaning and we find no fulfillment in our everyday lives. Without compassion, the thought of benefiting others, our hearts remain unfulfilled and it is very difficult for us to find satisfaction in whatever we do. No matter how much external wealth we have, if our hearts lack compassion, they are always empty; hollow inside.

If you check carefully, you will see that no matter how many things you have or how hard you try to achieve them, if there's no compassion in your heart, you never feel quite right. There's no peace in your heart, and deep within, you always feel that there's something missing.

The best way to give meaning to your life is to make it beneficial for others by having compassion for them. That's also the best way to find peace, happiness, fulfillment and satisfaction in your own life. But compassion for others does not only bring you peace and happiness right now, every moment of your present life. Living your life for others also offers you the best possible future. And even at that most critical juncture, the end of your life, when your consciousness separates from your body, compassion makes your death happy, peaceful and satisfying. Moreover, your peaceful, happy death, makes others happy too. Your friends and family can rejoice. You become an inspiration, an example of hope and courage. They see that their own deaths could also be happy.

Even if you have realized the wisdom directly perceiving the very nature of phenomena—the ultimate nature of the I and mind—if you have no compassion, no good heart, the most you can achieve is simply the nirvana of the Lesser Vehicle path, the sorrowless state for yourself alone; you cannot achieve full enlightenment. You still have the hallucination of the dualistic view. There are still subtle negative imprints on your mental continuum that prevent you from seeing directly all existence, the emptiness of all phenomena—all absolute and conventional truths together.

THE PURIFYING POWER OF COMPASSION

With compassion for others, leading your life for the benefit of others, you collect incredible merit. As the great bodhisattva pandit Shantideva said in the first chapter of his *Guide to the Bodhisattva's Life* (*Bodhicharyavatara*), when describing the benefits of bodhicitta, "Bodhicitta is the most powerful purifier of defilements, negative karma." There are a few stanzas where Shantideva talks about how powerful bodhicitta is in purifying negative karma.

He continues, "Like relying on a very powerful person when you want to be saved from danger, relying on bodhicitta, practicing bodhicitta, the good heart, for just a minute, even a second, purifies very powerful, inexhaustible, negative karma. Why, then, would the conscientious not entrust themselves to bodhicitta?" [Chapter 1, verse 13.]

If you have compassion in your everyday life, you collect the most extensive merit and purify much negative karma in a very short time. Many lifetimes, many eons, of negative karma get purified. That helps you to realize emptiness. How? To realize emptiness, you need much merit and great purification. For example, to realize a million dollar project, you need a million dollars. Similarly, to realize emptiness, you need a vast accumulation of merit. By practicing compassion, benefiting others, you accumulate great merit, and the realization of emptiness comes by the way.

Longdrol Lama Rinpoche, a great yogi from Sera-je Monastery who often saw Tara, the embodiment of all the buddhas' holy actions, said that she advised him to practice *tong-len*. This practice involves your taking other sentient beings' suffering and its cause onto yourself, destroying your ego, and giving your body, happiness, merit and everything else to other sentient beings, dedicating everything to others, causing them to receive whatever they need, as a result of which they actualize the path of method and wisdom and become enlightened. Tara told Longdrol Lama Rinpoche, "If you practice tong-len, taking and giving, the realization of emptiness will come by the way."

But that's not all. Through compassion, you not only realize emptiness; you also achieve full enlightenment, the total cessation of all mistakes of mind, all defilements, and the complete achievement of all realizations.

UNIVERSAL RESPONSIBILITY

If you don't have compassion, all you have is a self-centered mind. Due to that, anger, jealousy, desire and other such emotional thoughts arise. These negative thoughts then make you harm other sentient beings directly or indirectly, from life to life. You, one person with a negative attitude, inflict harm on all sentient beings. That's very dangerous. By comparison, even if all sentient beings get angry at, harm or even kill you, that's nothing. You are just one person; your importance is nothing. You are just one living being.

Therefore, it is essential, extremely important, that you, this one person, change your negative attitude and transform your mind into compassion, bodhicitta, in this life, immediately—*now*. Why? Because this life gives you every opportunity to do so. From beginningless rebirths up to now, you have not changed your attitude of self-cherishing—the source of all the problems and suffering that you yourself experience, and the source of your giving many problems and much harm to numberless other living beings—into the attitude of cherishing and benefiting others—the source of all peace and happiness for both yourself and numberless other living beings. You have not changed your ego, your self-centered mind, the thought of seeking happiness for only yourself, into the loving compassionate thought of bodhicitta. In this life, however, you can.

From your own side you have received the precious human body that has eight freedoms and ten richnesses. Furthermore, you have met not only a qualified virtuous friend who shows you virtue—the unmistaken cause of the happiness of future lives and the unmistaken path to liberation, freedom forever from samsara—but you have also met a qualified *Mahayana* virtuous friend, who reveals the complete, unmistaken path to full enlightenment, the non-abiding sorrowless state. You have met not only Buddhadharma but the Mahayana teaching. Even if you haven't met such a teacher yet, you have every opportunity to do so. Especially now, you have the opportunity of meeting the virtuous friend, His Holiness the Dalai Lama, who is proven by historical quotations of Guru Shakyamuni Buddha to be the Buddha of Compassion. This is like a dream come true; it is so difficult to express.

If you, one living being, develop compassion in your heart, you no longer give harm to numberless other living beings. You stop harming others. The absence of harm that your compassion brings numberless other sentient beings is peace and happiness. That is what they receive from you.

Not only that. As well as not receiving harm from you, others also receive benefit. Out of compassion, you help them. Thus, numberless other sentient beings receive much peace and happiness from you. All that is in your hands, because it is completely up to what you do with your own mind—whether you generate compassion for others or whether you don't. Numberless other sentient beings receiving harm or peace and happiness all depends on what you do with your own mind. It's all up to you. Therefore, each one of us here has complete responsibility for the peace and happiness of every single sentient being. Each of us has universal responsibility.

Therefore, twenty-four hours a day, from morning till night, as much as you can, you should put all your effort into generating the thought of universal responsibility: "I'm responsible for the peace and happiness of numberless other living beings; the purpose of my life is to bring happiness to other sentient beings." Get up in the morning with this attitude; get dressed with this attitude, this feeling of responsibility: "I'm responsible for all sentient beings' happiness; their peace and happiness is up to me." Know that this truly *is* the meaning of your life. Get dressed with this attitude, bathe with this attitude, eat breakfast with this attitude, go to work with this attitude.

WORKING WITH BODHICITTA

Also, during the day, while you are working, keep checking your attitude. It's not enough simply to leave home in the morning with this attitude. At work, check your motivation again and again, and repeatedly transform your attitude in this way. Keep generating the good heart; keep feeling responsible for all sentient beings' happiness, that it's up to you to cause it. Maintain a constant attitude of compassion, bodhicitta.

Examine your motivation again and again: "For whom am I doing this job? Am I doing it for myself or others?" If deep in your heart there's no continuity of the feeling that you are doing your job for others, if your attitude has changed, if you find that you're doing it for your own happiness, for yourself, then discard this attitude and replace it with the attitude that you are doing your job for the benefit of others, with compassion, the good heart, bodhicitta. Put as much effort as you possibly can into generating and maintaining the feeling that you're doing your job for the benefit others, not only for yourself.

Just because you're working for money doesn't mean that you're not benefiting others. If you use the money you earn to help others—for example, to help the sick or the poor, to spread Dharma or to help sentient beings in any other way—that's certainly for the benefit of others. If you are doing your job to save money so that you can do retreat or practice or study Dharma for the benefit other sentient beings, that's the right attitude; that's the attitude you should have. If you work and study so that you can live, but you live your life for the benefit of others; if you take care of yourself so that you can serve other sentient beings; if you feel, "I'm the servant of all sentient beings, serving to free them from suffering and bring them all happiness," you might be working in a regular job, but the work that you do is for others.

SLEEPING WITH BODHICITTA

When you go to bed, you should also sleep with a feeling of responsibility for the happiness of all sentient beings: "To free numberless other living beings from all their suffering and lead them to the great happiness of full enlightenment, I must first achieve enlightenment myself. In order to do so, I need to practice Dharma. To practice effectively, I need a long life and good health. Longevity and good health depend on sleep. Therefore, I'm now going to sleep."

The two things we spend most of our time doing are working and sleeping. Therefore, we need a good motivation for each, otherwise we are going to waste more than half of our lives. As the lam-rim teachings mention, we can spend almost half our lives sleeping. Therefore, it's very important to know not only how to make sleep virtuous, the cause of happiness, and not non-virtuous, the cause of suffering, but also how to make it the cause of numberless other living beings' happiness.

If you sleep with compassion, bodhicitta, the thought of benefiting others, your sleep becomes the cause of enlightenment, the cause of happiness of numberless other living beings. This is because anything you do with bodhicitta only benefits others, even before you become enlightened. As soon as you enter in the Mahayana path by developing bodhicitta, you begin to offer deep benefit to other sentient beings, and after you complete the path and achieve enlightenment, you bring numberless other sentient beings into full enlightenment.

Therefore, make sure that you put great effort into generating not only virtuous motivation but the very best Dharma attitude of compassion, bodhicitta, not only when you go to work but also when you go to sleep. In that way, your sleep becomes the best Dharma because it is unstained by the self-cherishing thought. So, that is the sutra way of sleeping, but there are also tantric meditations for both when you go to sleep and when you wake up, so that you awaken with that continuity. If you have received commentaries on the lower tantras or Highest Yoga Tantra, you should practice whatever you can remember.

TAKE REFUGE IN BODHICITTA

Our lives are so busy; we are preoccupied by many family and other obligations. When your life is so busy, there is no other refuge than your good heart. Your good heart is the most important thing in which to take refuge. Even though you might want to do long practices, sitting meditation, many prayers or retreat, your life is usually so busy that you don't have time. You have too many other obligations; you can't do everything that you'd like. If this is the case, your only refuge is your good heart, your compassion, the thought of benefiting others, bodhicitta. If you take refuge in that, if you can practice that, no matter how busy you are—even if you cannot do many hours of sitting meditation, prayers, preliminary practices and so forth, you will have no regrets over lost opportunities, now or in the future. In this life and in all future lives, you will go from happiness to happiness to enlightenment.

There are so many practices you can do—what's the most important? What's the most important thing to practice in life? I would say that it's the good heart, your very precious thought of loving kindness, compassion; the thought of benefiting others, bodhicitta. That is the best meditation, the best Dharma practice.

As Shantideva also said when talking about the benefits of bodhicitta in the *Bodhicharyavatara*, "After checking for many eons, the buddhas discovered that bodhicitta is the most beneficial thing for sentient beings." [Chapter 1, verse 7.]

This quotation explains what's best for you. That means that bodhicitta is the best thing for you too. What's the best way to take care of yourself? What's the best thing for your own well-being? It's bodhicitta. The buddhas' discovery applies equally to you.

There are so many problems in life—cancer, AIDS, relationship problems, being in debt, not having enough money, job problems such as other people being jealous of you or interfering with your work or being unable to find a job. There are so many problems. But the one answer that takes care of everything, the one solution to all your life's problems, the one thing that fulfills all your wishes, is again *your* mind, *your* good heart, *your* bodhicitta.

If you have a good heart, you don't give harm others; you always help others with their problems, whatever they are. That causes you to have a long and healthy life. The lam-rim teachings talk about the eight ripened qualities of a good rebirth [see *Liberation in the Palm of Your Hand,* p. 460]. One of these is a long life, the cause of which is explained as saving or sparing the lives of others, animal or human; for example, giving them food, medicine, clothing or helping them in various other ways [*Liberation,* p. 462].

Therefore, in your everyday life, try with a good heart to benefit others as much as possible. If you can do this, whether you are offering others great service or small, you're continuously creating the cause of your own success—wealth, long life, good health, everything. Your actions are harmonious with such results. Thus, your good heart fulfills all your wishes for *any* happiness, including the highest, peerless happiness of full enlightenment. Actions done with a good heart are never non-virtuous, only virtuous. Actions done with a good heart only benefit and never harm others. Therefore, when you act with a good heart, you never create the cause for sicknesses, only health. Your wish to benefit others is a healthy mind. That healthy mind makes your body healthy.

OVERCOMING ILLNESS WITH BODHICITTA

Nowadays, many highly intelligent Western doctors, psychologists and scientists have checked and proven with their wisdom that diseases such as cancer come from the individual's own negative attitude. Cancer comes from the negative mind. Therefore, the way to heal cancer is to have a positive attitude, a pure mind.

For example, in Singapore, there was a Chinese Dharma

student who had AIDS. He informed his guru, a very high lama called Ratö Rinpoche, who lived in Dharamsala. Rinpoche sent this student instructions on how to do the special bodhicitta practice that I mentioned before, tong-len, as a remedy, a method for him to practice. So, he practiced for four days and then went to the hospital for a check-up, where the doctors told him, "You no longer have AIDS." After four days they found no trace of AIDS. When I heard this, I thought he must have spent many hours a day practicing tong-len, so I asked him, "How much did you practice?" "Four minutes a day," he said!

He practiced only four minutes a day, but during that time his compassion was unbelievably strong. There was no space in his mind for his own AIDS. His only concern was for the many other people who have AIDS. During those four minutes a day he felt so much compassion that tears poured down his cheeks. He felt it was unbearable that other sentient beings should suffer from AIDS. Why could the doctors find no trace of AIDS after he had practiced for only four days? Because even though he had practiced meditation for only a few minutes a day, the meditation that he did practice had the power of an atomic bomb. His compassion for others was so powerful that it purified his mind of vast amounts of negative karma.

Do you remember the quote from Shantideva that I mentioned before, how bodhicitta purifies inexhaustible heavy negative karma? That's what happened here. The principal cause of AIDS is negative imprints left on the mental continuum by past negative actions. This student's compassion was so powerful that it neutralized the karmic cause of his disease.

In the same way, meditation can also cure cancer. The same reasoning applies. In my own experience, five or six people with terminal cancer completely recovered by reciting the mantras of various buddhas with whom they had a connection. They had been told by their doctors that they were going to die, that they had only two or three months to live, but by purifying the principal cause of their cancer, which was in their mind, they completely overcame their disease. Mantra recitation can also heal other sicknesses, such as heart disease.

I heard about a person in Spain who had a very serious heart disease. His heart was enlarged and the doctors gave him only a short time to live. The geshe at our Nagarjuna Center in Barcelona advised him to recite Guru Shakyamuni Buddha's mantra, TAYATHA OM MUNE MUNE MAHA MUNAYE SOHA, 300,000 times. Geshe-la gave him a big number to do! Anyway, he followed Geshe-la's advice, and his heart decreased in size until it became normal. I was also told by a famous Spanish musician about someone else who had recovered from AIDS through meditation, but I don't know the details of that case.

However, what I'm trying to emphasize here is that generating a good heart is the best way of taking care of your health.

Nowadays, there are many new diseases occurring, many new dangers to life. The best way to avoid experiencing those sicknesses is not to create their cause. Thus, a good heart is the best protection from disease. And, should you contract any disease, developing a good heart is also the best way to overcome it.

EATING WITH BODHICITTA

Before eating breakfast, lunch or dinner, remember to feel, "I am responsible for the happiness of all sentient beings; this is the purpose of my life. In order to fulfill this purpose, I need to be healthy and live long. Therefore, I'm going to eat this food." In this way, every time you eat or drink, it becomes service for all sentient beings.

When you eat and drink with bodhicitta, it becomes the cause of happiness for all sentient beings. At the beginning, when you generate bodhicitta, you collect skies of good luck, merit, good karma, and after that, every single mouthful of food and drink you take also becomes the cause of your enlightenment and the happiness of all sentient beings.

If you eat with the thought of benefiting all sentient beings, the more food there is on your plate, the bigger the pile of food you eat, the more good karma you collect. With every mouthful, you collect skies of merit. The more hours you eat, that much richer, more meaningful, your life becomes.

EVERYTHING YOU DO CAN BECOME DHARMA

Similarly, as I mentioned before, if you do your job with bodhicitta, the more hours you work, the more causes of liberation and enlightenment you create. Incidentally, your job becomes a means for achieving happiness in future lives and liberation from samsara. You find peace and happiness in the present moment and, more importantly, you create the best possible future for yourself and others. In this way, everything you do becomes Dharma. Your daily life and Dharma become one. Twenty-four hours a day, your life is integrated with the best kind of meditation, integrated with Dharma.

Even if you know by heart all 84,000 teachings of the Buddha, all the sutras and tantras, the hundreds of volumes of the Buddhist canon, and can explain and teach it all, if in your daily life you don't protect your mind from the delusions, the disturbing, obscuring thoughts, you're not practicing Dharma. Why? Because the definition of Dharma is that which is a remedy for delusion, like medicine is a remedy for sickness. For your actions to become Dharma, they have to be an antidote to your delusions. Therefore, if you don't protect your mind from delusion, if you constantly allow your mind to be controlled by delusion, to be overwhelmed by delusion, if you become a slave to your delusions, to your real enemy—ignorance, anger, attachment and so forth—if you don't practice controlling your delusions, protecting your mind from them, freeing your mind from delusions, nothing you do becomes Dharma; you never create the cause of happiness.

On the other hand, whenever in your everyday life there's the danger of delusion arising and you protect yourself from it, at that time you are practicing Dharma. Whenever you free your mind from delusion, prevent even one delusion from arising and controlling or overwhelming you, at that time you are practicing actual Dharma.

Therefore, if you can use whatever education you have had—

Dharma or any other kind—to protect yourself, to keep your mind free from delusion, and to benefit others as well, to bring true peace and happiness to others, then all of it, not only the Dharma that you have studied, will have become extremely meaningful. All those years that you put into educating yourself will have really paid off.

THE FOUR WAYS OF BENEFITING OTHERS

I mentioned before that benefiting others, making your body, speech and mind beneficial for others, is the purpose of life. However, there are different levels of benefit that you can offer. The first is bringing others the happiness of this life. More important than that is causing them to have happiness in all their future lives. Then, even more important than that, is leading other sentient beings to complete liberation, freedom forever from the entire round of suffering, the cycle of death and rebirth and the three kinds of suffering. The three sufferings are the suffering of pain; the suffering of change, temporary samsaric pleasure; and the suffering that is the basis of the other two, pervasive compounding suffering, the aggregates that are under the control of karma and delusion, and the contaminated seed of disturbing thoughts, which is both the container of this life's suffering and the basis of future lives' suffering. The benefit of bringing others to total liberation is much more important than the first two.

However, the highest, most important benefit that you can

possibly offer other sentient beings is causing them to achieve full enlightenment, complete attainment of all the qualities of cessation and realization.

In order to do this work for all sentient beings perfectly, with no mistake, first you need to achieve full enlightenment yourself. Enlightenment doesn't occur without cause. You need to actualize the three levels of the path to enlightenment—the graduated path of the being of greatest capability, which depends on actualizing the graduated path traveled in common with the being of intermediate capability, which depends on the actualizing the preliminary graduated path traveled in common with the being of least capability. Success in all this—from the beginning of the lam-rim, realization of the perfect human rebirth, up to enlightenment—depends completely on the root of the path, guru devotion.

GURU DEVOTION

Proper guru devotion means seeing that your guru is buddha. Based on quotations of Buddha Vajradhara or Shakyamuni Buddha, logical reasoning and your personal experiences with your guru, the special qualities you have seen, you train your mind to look at your guru as buddha, free of all mistakes and complete in all qualities.

You must see as buddha all the teachers with whom you have established a Dharma connection. A Dharma connection is established when from your side you recognize the teacher as guru and yourself as disciple—even if all you have received from this teacher is the oral transmission of just one mantra or one verse of teaching—supporting this view with quotations of the Buddha, logical reasoning and your experience of the particular qualities you have seen within that teacher. In this way, then, you see your guru as buddha, as pure. Proper guru devotion, correct devotion to your virtuous friends, allows you to actualize successfully all the realizations of the steps of the path to enlightenment, from the perfect human rebirth up to buddhahood itself.

His Holiness the Dalai Lama mentioned analysis of the guru's qualifications. The qualification needed to teach the Lesser Vehicle path is accomplishment in the three higher trainings—morality, concentration and wisdom. In order to teach the Mahayana, the teacher needs more than that; he or she should have the ten qualities mentioned in Maitreya Buddha's teaching *Ornament for the Mahayana Sutras* (*Do-de-gyän; Mahayanasutralamkarakarika*). I'm not going to translate these word-for-word but will just mention their meaning [see *Liberation in the Palm of Your Hand*, pp. 272-3].

First [1-3], a Mahayana guru should also be accomplished in the three higher trainings. Moreover, since we are talking about practicing Dharma, [4] the teacher should have more good qualities than you do and greater knowledge of Dharma. [5] He should have perseverance and [6] his holy mind should be enriched with scriptural understanding, having received the lineage of the teachings.

Also, [7] your teacher should have realized emptiness. Now, I have already mentioned that the guru should be accomplished in the three higher trainings, one of which is the training in higher wisdom, so why is the realization of emptiness mentioned again here? The difference is that here, the realization of emptiness refers to the Prasangika Madhyamika view—the view of emptiness according to the higher of the two Madhyamika schools, the Prasangika school. That particular view of emptiness is the only one that can eradicate the actual root of samsara, the specific ignorance that causes all the other delusions and karma and the suffering that sentient beings experience. There's only one root of samsara—that specific ignorance can be cut only by the Prasangika view of emptiness and not by the view of any other school. That is the seventh quality your teacher should possess.

The final three qualities are [8] skill in explaining Dharma, [9] compassion for the students, and [10] not being lazy when it comes to giving teachings and guiding disciples. A guru should not have the attitude, "It's too difficult" or "I can't be bothered teaching." Even if the teacher doesn't have all ten qualities, he should have as many as possible.

The qualities of a guru are also mentioned in the *Fifty Verses of the Guru Devotion* [verses 7-9; see also Lama Tsong Khapa's commentary to this text, *The Fulfillment of All Hopes*, pp. 40-48] and the *Guru Puja*, in the section praising the qualities of the guru—having a well-disciplined body, speech and mind; great wisdom and tolerance; a sincere, straight mind, without the cunning of hiding one's own mistakes; and the ten inner qualities required to teach Highest Yoga Tantra and the ten outer qualities required to teach the lower tantras [verse 45].

YOUR TEACHER MUST EMPHASIZE MORALITY

However, whether you can see all those qualities or not, the essence is to have a teacher who emphasizes morality. The one basic, important, fundamental quality to look for is the teacher's emphasis on morality—pratimoksha, bodhisattva and, for those who practice tantra, tantric vows. A teacher who does not stress moral conduct cannot even lead disciples to good rebirths in their next lives, let alone to liberation from samsara and enlightenment.

I have always admired Geshe Michael Roach in this. I have heard from many students that Geshe-la always teaches the pratimoksha and bodhisattva vows and makes his students memorize them. He makes sure that everyone understands and can explain the vows they hold.

These are very essential, fundamental practices. Without the practice of morality, there's no enlightenment, no liberation from samsara, not even good rebirths in future lives. I'm not saying that in order to receive a good rebirth you have to take all three levels of vow, but in order to receive a good rebirth you must at least keep the pratimoksha vows.

Death can come at any time; any minute, you can die. Therefore, if you are going to die today, at least you must be sure of getting a good rebirth; you must be completely sure that you are not going to fall into the hell, hungry ghost or animal realms, where you will be completely overwhelmed by suffering.

Even when we're sick or the weather is hot, we human beings can't meditate. If we compare our lives to those of sentient beings in the lower realms, we have incredible freedom, incredibly luxurious lives. Nevertheless, when we experience problems, we cannot practice Dharma. Beings in the lower realms are totally overwhelmed by suffering and have no opportunity to practice. Therefore, you have to guarantee that when you die—this year, this month, this week or even today—you will not be reborn in the lower realms. You must make sure you receive a good rebirth. For this, you have to prepare right now.

The best preparation, the main cause for receiving a good rebirth, is practicing morality. That doesn't necessarily mean becoming a monk or nun. There are lay vows. You can take the eight precepts, the five precepts or even fewer than five. Of the five, you can take one, two, three or four; whatever you feel you can manage. However, if you keep purely whatever vows you take and die with them intact, the immediate benefit is that you will definitely receive a good rebirth in your next life. Then, in that life, you can practice Dharma again, and in that way, from life to life, go from happiness to happiness, all the way to enlightenment.

Therefore, emphasis on morality to inspire morality in the disciple is a very important quality to look for in a teacher. That's why I rejoice whenever I hear how Geshe Michael Roach always emphasizes and teaches his students the importance of moral discipline. It gives you incredible freedom. If you take precepts and live in them purely, you are giving yourself freedom—liberation from samsaric suffering, and enlightenment.

It is also extremely important for your guru to have maintained pure samaya, a good connection, with his or her own gurus, because the extent to which a teacher can benefit his disciples and cause them to have realizations depends on his own samaya with his gurus. If you devote yourself correctly to a virtuous friend whose samaya is good, even if he gives you only a few words of instruction, because of the purity and power of his samaya, those words can have an incredible effect on your mind. They can generate strong feelings of compassion, renunciation, impermanence and death, or even precipitate a realization of emptiness. If your guru does not have pure samaya, there's always the danger that you will receive mental pollution or make the same mistakes with your gurus as he did.

THE NINE ATTITUDES OF GURU DEVOTION
(See Appendix 1)

Now I'd like to read the nine attitudes of guru devotion that Lama Tsong Khapa explained in the *Lam-rim Chen-mo*, which I translated during the Vajrasattva retreat at Land of Medicine Buddha in early 1999. I'm not going to give much explanation here; I just want to read through it. Those of you who have studied this subject will understand it; those who haven't will get some idea of it. Reading this teaching is very helpful, especially if your mind is experiencing difficulties with your guru. It's like an atomic bomb; it makes all those difficult thoughts vanish completely.

What follows is not from the *Lam-rim Chen-mo* itself, but these nine attitudes are mentioned there. The text, *Practicing Guru Devotion with the Nine Attitudes*, was actually written by Shabkar

Tsogdrug Rangdrol, a Nyingma lama who received teachings from Gelug lamas who taught the lam-rim in the way that Lama Tsong Khapa did. Shabkar's presentation is so effective that I translated it.

"I am requesting the kind lord root guru,
Who is more extraordinary than all the buddhas—
Please bless me to be able to devote myself to the qualified
    lord guru
With great respect, in all my future lifetimes.

"By realizing that the root of happiness and goodness
Is correctly devoting myself to the kind lord guru,
Who is the foundation of all good qualities,
I shall devote myself to him with great respect,
Not forsaking him even at the cost of my life."

Thinking of the importance of the qualified guru,
Allow yourself to enter under his control.

Well, I said I wasn't going to talk, but sorry, it says "control," so I think I have to say something, because nobody likes to be controlled! Especially in the West. Nobody wants to be controlled by anybody. Not even by mosquitoes! Anyway, I'm joking. But if you don't understand what this verse means, you might take it the wrong way when you hear that you should put yourself under your guru's control. However, a simple example will clarify this.

If you put yourself under the control of a good friend and

follow that person's advice, you too can become good person, but if you let yourself be controlled by a bad friend, you might become a bad person yourself. If you do what a good friend says, you don't create problems for yourself or others; you only make others happy. In *Liberation in the Palm of Your Hand*, Pabongka Dechen Nyingpo talks about two people, one of whom was an alcoholic, the other who didn't drink. The drinker went to Reting Monastery and became a teetotaler. The non-drinker went to Lhasa, where, influenced by others, he began drinking and became an alcoholic. Each man became the complete opposite of what he was before, due to the influence of the type of friend he followed.

If you listen to the advice of the Buddha—who has only compassion for sentient beings and no trace of self-centered mind; who is perfect in power, wisdom and compassion; whose holy mind is omniscient—all you get is benefit. Putting yourself under the control of the Buddha brings you every happiness up to that of enlightenment. You get happiness now and every possible future happiness. Similarly, if you put yourself under the control of a virtuous friend, you get the same benefits as you do from putting yourself under the control of the Buddha. There's only benefit and not the slightest harm.

Now, relating this teaching to those of us who met the Dharma a long time ago, if we had been under the control of our gurus from that time forth, we would have achieved many realizations by now. We could have realized guru devotion, renunciation, bodhicitta and emptiness; we could have received realizations of tantra; we could have been totally liberated from samsara. We might even have become enlightened. At the very least, we would have received some lam-rim realizations. But none of this has happened because we have not opened our hearts to our guru; we have not put ourselves under the control of our virtuous friend. Because of this mistake, our minds are totally devoid of any realization whatsoever.

The first two attitudes are:

1. Be like an obedient son—
Act exactly in accordance with the guru's advice.

2. Even when maras, evil friends and the like
Try to split you from the guru,
Be like a vajra—
Inseparable forever.

The yogi Drubkang Tsangpa Gyari, a Kagyu lama, said, "If something goes wrong in your relationship with your guru, even if all sentient beings become your friend, what's the use?" In other words, if something damages your connection with your guru—the auspiciousness of the relationship or your samaya—then even if all living beings become your friend, what's the use? What can they do? What can you do? Since something has gone wrong in your relationship with your guru, until you repair that relationship, until you do something to restore it, even if everybody becomes your friend, you cannot achieve liberation from samsara, enlightenment, or even realizations of the path.

I don't remember the next verse of this lama's teaching word-for-word, but the meaning is that if you maintain a good connection with your guru, if nothing goes wrong with it, then even if all living beings desert you or become your enemy, it doesn't matter.

Ordinary people would think that everybody becoming your friend or enemy is a big thing, but in Dharma practice, once you have made a connection with a guru and not made any mistakes in the relationship, that's all that matters. Even if everybody becomes your enemy, it's of no consequence, because from the foundation of that good relationship you can attain all realizations and enjoy every success up to enlightenment, and after that, you can benefit all sentient beings by enlightening them too. That's the meaning of this great yogi's teaching.

3. Whenever the guru gives you work,
No matter how heavy the burden,
Be like the earth—
Bear it all.

4. When devoting yourself to the guru,
Whatever suffering occurs,
Be like a mountain—
Immovable.

Here, suffering means hardship or problems, and when this happens, your mind should remain immovable and not be upset or discouraged.

5. Even if you are given all the difficult tasks,
Be like the servant of a king—
Perform them with an undisturbed mind.

6. Abandon pride.
Be like a sweeper—
Hold yourself lower than the guru.

I'm not sure how this comes across in the West, but in the East, a sweeper is the lowest of the low. In the West, people like to think that everybody's equal, but in the East, a sweeper is regarded as very low.

7. No matter how difficult or heavy the burden,
Be like a rope—
Hold the guru's work with joy.

8. Even when the guru criticizes, provokes or ignores you,
Be like a faithful dog—
Never respond with anger.

No matter how much a dog gets beaten by its master, it always shows respect and never gets angry. When it sees its master coming, it starts wagging its tail and runs to lick him, showing much happiness.

9. Be like a boat—
Never be upset to come or go for the guru
At any time.

"O glorious and precious root guru,
Please bless me to be able to practice in this way.
From now on, in all my future lifetimes,
May I be able to devote myself to the guru like this."

If you recite these words aloud and reflect on their meaning in your mind, you will have the good fortune of being able to devote yourself correctly to the precious guru from life to life, in all your future lifetimes.

If you offer service and respect and make offerings to the precious guru with these nine attitudes in mind, even if you do not practice intentionally, you will develop many good qualities, collect extensive merit and quickly achieve full enlightenment.

This last verse explains that even if you don't study or do any particular practices, like preliminaries, retreats and so forth—in other words, you don't practice intentionally—if you devote yourself to your virtuous friend correctly with thought and action, you will naturally develop many good qualities, constantly collect extensive merit and quickly achieve full enlightenment.

Therefore, each time you do even one thing your guru told

you, you take a step closer to enlightenment. Whenever you do something that your guru has advised, it becomes great purification. Many lifetimes' heavy negative karma gets purified, you collect inconceivable merit and you get closer and closer to enlightenment.

For example, even cleaning your guru's room. Each time you clean it, you get closer and closer to enlightenment. This is because, of all the powerful objects, your guru is the most powerful; more powerful than the numberless buddhas and bodhisattvas. This power comes into being the moment that person becomes your guru. The moment you make a Dharma connection with the recognition of another person as guru and yourself as disciple—whether from their side the other person is enlightened or not, a bodhisattva or not a bodhisattva—that person becomes the most powerful person in your life; more powerful than all the buddhas and bodhisattvas. Therefore, whatever service you offer, even one cleaning of your guru's room, purifies much negative karma and brings you closer to enlightenment. Therefore, you should remember that each time you offer service to your guru, whatever it is, you are purifying your mind and getting closer to enlightenment.

Towards the end of his life, Lama Atisha showed the aspect of sickness and incontinence and made pipi and kaka in his bed because he was unable to get up and go to the toilet. His translator, Drom Tönpa, with no thought of dirtiness, offered service by bathing Lama Atisha and cleaning his bed. As a result, Drom Tönpa purified so many karmic obscurations that he developed the clairvoyance of being able to read the minds of even tiny creatures, such as ants and worms, that were as far away as an eagle can fly in eighteen days.

By serving your guru, realizations just come. The potential of all realizations is there within your mind. You just need purification to reveal them. The more you purify, the more realizations you receive.

Pabongka Dechen Nyingpo, the author of *Liberation in the Palm of Your Hand*, had a disciple who couldn't read. I think his name was Jamyang. He didn't even know the alphabet. Before Pabongka Dechen Nyingpo passed away, he told this attendant that eventually he would be able to read the entire *Guru Puja* by himself, without being taught. And that's exactly what happened. After going into exile from Tibet, Jamyang finished up at the refugee camp at Buxa, where I lived for eight years and received philosophical teachings from my three gurus, Geshe Rabten Rinpoche, Lama Yeshe and another lama, also called Gen Yeshe. During the British rule of India, Buxa was the concentration camp where Mahatma Gandhi-ji and Prime Minister Nehru were imprisoned. Nehru-ji's place of imprisonment became the Sera Monastery prayer hall and Gandhi-ji's, a nunnery.

At Buxa, the incarnate lamas lived on a mountain high above the rest of the camp. The abbot and main teacher at Kopan Monastery, Lama Lhundrub, who supervises the education and discipline of the three hundred Kopan monks, used to live up there in the same building as Pabongka Dechen Nyingpo's incarnation, where the attendant Jamyang also lived. When

Jamyang first arrived at Buxa, he couldn't read a thing, but suddenly one day he was able to read the entire *Guru Puja*. He himself told Lama Lhundrub that Pabongka Dechen Nyingpo had predicted that this would happen.

If you purify your mind, realizations will come. What you need is purification and the most powerful purification is correct devotion to your virtuous friend; obeying your guru's advice. The best way to devote yourself to your virtuous friend is through practicing his teachings, the second is by offering service and respect—cleaning your guru's place, cooking for him and so forth—and the third is by offering material things, if you have them to offer [see *Liberation*, p. 299 ff.].

The story goes that Lama Atisha's cook, who spent all his time cooking for Lama Atisha and never had time to meditate, had much greater realizations than the Kadampa geshe Gombawa, another of Lama Atisha's disciples, who spent all his time meditating in a cave. So that's how it is, and now it's time to finish.

CONCLUSION

I would like to thank you all very much for giving me this opportunity to share something with you. I hope that there's been at least some small benefit from my mumbling.

The opportunity we have to learn Dharma in this life is great; we can't be sure that we will get such a good opportunity again in future lifetimes. Especially if you have the opportunity to study Dharma in your own language without having to go through a translator, you should take it. There are many difficulties when the Dharma comes through translation—missing words, incorrect meanings, it doesn't come out exactly as presented by the lama, it doesn't convey exactly the same feeling in others' minds—but you don't have to put up with all these difficulties.

Those who are able to receive realizations of what the Dharma texts talk about are those who have proper guru devotion; they're the ones who can achieve enlightenment in one life. Those who have realized guru devotion, who have correctly devoted themselves to their virtuous friend, can become enlightened in one brief lifetime of this degenerate age. It's the same thing as regards all the realizations of the path to enlightenment. Without guru devotion, no matter how many Dharma words you learn, they're all dry. However, if you have such strong guru devotion that whenever you simply mention your guru's name, tears come to your eyes, you will be able to gain realizations of bodhicitta, emptiness and everything else without much difficulty, in this very life.

DEDICATION

Dedicate the merits collected tonight by listening to and explaining the Dharma, and all the past, present and future merit collected by yourselves and others as well, for the Buddha of Compassion, His Holiness the Dalai Lama, and all other holy beings to have stable lives, for all their holy wishes to succeed immediately and for the sangha—the sangha in general and the Western sangha in particular—to be able to complete their scriptural understanding and realizations of the whole path in this very lifetime by receiving all the conditions necessary to do so.

Dedicate for Geshe Michael Roach to have a long life and for all his wishes to succeed immediately, for all the students who are studying here also to have long lives and to be able to completely actualize Lama Tsong Khapa's stainless path of unified sutra and tantra in this very lifetime and for their Arizona retreat center and all other projects to succeed immediately by receiving everything necessary to do so. Pray for everyone who comes onto that land, from that moment on, to never ever again be reborn in the lower realms, to be immediately liberated from all disease, spirit harm, negative karma and all defilement, to be able to find unshakable faith in refuge and karma, and to be able to actualize bodhicitta, realize emptiness, and achieve enlightenment as quickly as possible.

Please dedicate for the five-hundred-foot Maitreya Buddha statue in Bodhgaya to be completed without any obstacles and to be most beneficial for all sentient beings by causing them to generate bodhicitta in their minds and achieve enlightenment as quickly as possible.

Next, I would like to thank Geshe-la and his students from the bottom of my heart for their sponsoring a silver-paged copy of the *Diamond Sutra* adorned with gold, diamonds and rubies for inclusion in the five-hundred-foot Maitreya Buddha statue.

According to Vajrayana, statues are normally filled with mantras. But this statue is five-hundred-feet high—it would be like filling the whole sky with mantras, it's so huge. Therefore, our idea is to make different temples inside the statue. There will be a Twenty-one Taras temple, a Medicine Buddha temple, a Sixteen Arhats temple and so forth. There will be various temples dedicated exclusively in that way. At the heart of the statue will be a temple containing Buddha's and many other relics, so that people can prostrate, circumambulate and make offerings to them.

I would like there to be another temple containing all Lord Buddha's Prajnaparamita teachings, written with gold ink on special paper. I have already started writing *The Sutra of the Perfection of Wisdom in Eight Thousand Verses* using gold from Nepal. Even while traveling, I keep writing. At the rate I'm going, it's going to take me a few more years to finish. This temple will also contain other texts, such as the *Heart Sutra*, written in gold and silver and decorated with coral, pearls and other precious stones, for people to prostrate to, circumambulate, make light and water bowl offerings to and rejoice over.

Anyway, I don't want to keep on talking, but there is just one more thing I want to say. The sutra text *Condensed Precious Qualities* says—and I'm not going to quote it verbatim but just explain the meaning—that if you fill world systems equal in number to the grains of sand in the Ganges, that huge long Indian river, with stupas made not of bricks and mortar but of the seven types of precious substances and containing Buddha's relics, and then all the sentient beings living in that vast number of world systems make offerings to those precious stupas, the great merit thus generated is still inferior to that created by writing even in black ink just one *Prajnaparamita* text. Therefore, your sponsoring a silver and gold edition of the *Diamond Sutra* adorned with jewels is unbelievably meritorious. So, I just wanted to point that out and rejoice in your great merit.

Whenever I write another bit of this Prajnaparamita text, I try my best to dedicate the merit to world peace, and pray, "Wherever this text may be—in whatever universe, world or area—may there be no war, disease or natural disaster such as fire, flood, earthquake and so forth, and may everybody there realize bodhicitta, the good heart, enjoy perfect peace and happiness, and as quickly as possible realize the wisdom directly perceiving emptiness, cease all their defilements and achieve enlightenment."

Due to the past, present and future merit collected by ourselves and all the buddhas, bodhisattvas and other sentient beings, which are totally nonexistent from their own side, may the I, which is totally nonexistent from its own side, achieve Guru Shakyamuni Buddha's enlightenment, which is also totally nonexistent from its own side, and lead all sentient beings, who are also totally nonexistent from their own side, to that enlightenment, which is also totally nonexistent from its own side, by myself alone, who is also totally nonexistent from its own side.

Finally, please dedicate that you, your family members and all other sentient beings may completely actualize Lama Tsong Khapa's stainless path of unified sutra and tantra in this very lifetime and be able to meet this teaching in all lifetimes and cause it to flourish and spread in all directions.

Colophon

This teaching was given in the East Village, New York City, on 13 August, 1999, at the request of Geshe Michael Roach and his students, on the auspicious occasion of His Holiness the Dalai Lama's visit to New York.

REFERENCES

Shantideva, *A Guide to the Bodhisattva's Way of Life*, Stephen Batchelor (tr.). Dharamsala: LTWA, 1979.

Pabongka Rinpoche, *Liberation in the Palm of Your Hand*, Michael Richards (tr.). Boston: Wisdom Publications, 1991.

Asvaghosa, *Fifty Verses of Guru Devotion*, LTWA (tr.). Dharamsala: LTWA, 1975.

Tsong Khapa, *The Fulfillment of All Hopes*, Gareth Sparham (tr.). Boston: Wisdom Publications, 1999.

Matthieu Ricard (tr.), *The Life of Shabkar*. Albany: SUNY Press, 1994.

Lama Zopa Rinpoche, *Teachings from the Vajrasattva Retreat*. Boston: Lama Yeshe Wisdom Archive, 2000.

Two

How to Make Each Moment of Our Lives Meaningful

It all depends on motivation

It is extremely important for us to know how best to lead our daily lives. This depends upon our knowing what is a spiritual action and what is not, the difference between what is Dharma and what is not Dharma. The benefits of having this knowledge are incredible, infinite.

Take, for example, four people reciting the same Buddhist prayer. The first recites it with the motivation of achieving enlightenment for the sake of all sentient beings. Because of this motivation, the recitation does become a cause of enlightenment, not only for the person doing the recitation but for all sentient beings.

The second person recites the prayer motivated by the desire for his or her own liberation from samsara. This action does not become a cause for the enlightenment of all sentient beings but for the everlasting happiness of liberation of that person alone.

The third person recites the prayer with the motivation of receiving happiness in future lives. The result of this is neither enlightenment nor liberation, but simply happiness in a future life.

The fourth person, however, recites the prayer motivated by attachment clinging to the happiness of this life. Even though it is a Dharma prayer, a teaching of the Buddha, this person's recitation is not a Dharma action, not a spiritual practice. It is a worldly dharma, the cause of suffering. Why? Because the motivation of attachment clinging to this life has the negative effect of disturbing the mind, of making it unpeaceful. Therefore, such motivation is labeled non-virtuous, as is the action itself. They are non-virtuous because they result in suffering.

Lama Atisha, the great Indian yogi and pandit who was invited to Tibet to re-establish the pure Dharma, was asked by his translator Drom Tönpa, himself an emanation of Avalokiteshvara, "What are the results of actions done simply for this life?" Lama Atisha replied that such actions cause unfortunate, suffering rebirths in the three lower realms—the hell, hungry ghost or animal realms.

Although I am using the action of reciting a prayer as an example, what we have to realize is that the above applies to all our actions throughout the twenty-four hours of each day—walking, sitting, sleeping, eating, talking, working at our jobs—everything we do, even breathing. Every single action can become a cause of either enlightenment, liberation or happiness in future lives, or rebirth in the suffering lower realms. It all depends on our motivation.

For example, the simple action of drinking, swallowing just one mouthful of water, can become the cause of either enlightenment, liberation or happiness in future lives, or rebirth in the suffering lower realms. If you drink with a Dharma mind, that action of drinking becomes Dharma, the cause of happiness. If you drink with a worldly, non-Dharma mind, with attachment, or even worse, anger, this action is non-virtuous, a cause for rebirth in the lower realms.

Therefore, you should think like this: "If I drink water with bodhicitta motivation, no matter how many mouthfuls I take or how many glasses I drink, every single one becomes a cause of enlightenment, a cause of happiness for all sentient beings. If, however, I drink this water with attachment clinging to this life, then each mouthful, each glass, becomes only the cause of suffering—the unbearable suffering of the lower realms and all the problems experienced by human beings as well."

If I talk to you with the worldly mind of attachment clinging to this life, then for as many hours as I talk, every moment becomes the cause of unfortunate rebirths, the cause of suffering.

If you drive a car with the motivation of attachment clinging to this life, then for as long as you drive, it all becomes negative karma. If, however, you drive with positive motivation, there is no doubt that it all becomes the cause of happiness.

If you sleep with attachment clinging to this life, the longer you sleep, the more negative karma, the more causes of lower rebirths, you create.

It's the same when you write letters or books, read the newspaper or watch television—your motivation determines whether that action becomes Dharma, the cause of happiness, or negative karma, the cause of suffering.

When you go shopping, again, your motivation determines

whether it becomes the cause of enlightenment for other sentient beings, your own liberation or happiness in future lives, or the cause of suffering. If you shop with attachment clinging to this life, every time you buy something, it creates negative karma and is therefore not Dharma but the cause of suffering.

Similarly, when you work at your job, if the hours you spend working are motivated by bodhicitta, the determination to reach enlightenment for the benefit of all sentient beings, every moment becomes the cause of other sentient beings' happiness, but if you work with attachment clinging to this life, everything you do becomes the cause for you to suffer in the lower realms.

INTERNAL EDUCATION COMES FIRST

Whatever work you do, there are two things to learn. The first is how to do the actual work, how to do your job, which is what you learn in school and college. This is what most people in the world are educated to do. But that alone is not sufficient. As I have already mentioned, that is nowhere near enough to ensure that your actions serve as the unmistaken cause of happiness. Simply knowing how to do your job never solves your problems completely. Neglecting inner education, which teaches you the attitude with which you should perform your tasks and how to live your life, and focusing on outer education alone brings neither satisfaction nor fulfillment to your heart.

It is of the utmost importance that you understand how to use your mind correctly when you do the things you do. There is no other choice. Why? If, for example, you're working as a secretary or cooking with Dharma motivation—perhaps for your own happiness beyond this life or the happiness of others—then whatever you do becomes the cause of happiness, a good rebirth in the next life, the body of the happy transmigrator. If, even better, you have bodhicitta motivation, the determination to reach enlightenment for the sake of all sentient beings, then the secretarial work, cooking or whatever else you do becomes the cause of all sentient beings' enlightenment.

Thus you can see that internal work—how to use your mind, how to motivate your actions—is far more important than external work, because it is this that determines whether what you do becomes the cause of happiness or the cause of suffering. Instruction in this, how to use your mind correctly, is what's missing from our schools' curricula. How to live intelligently is not taught in schools, colleges or universities.

Because you get paid for doing your job, it appears to be the cause of happiness and you believe it to be so. In reality, no matter how perfectly you do your job, how skilled you are or how many billions of dollars you make, since you are doing it out of worldly motivation, attachment clinging to this life, the work you do can never become the cause of happiness but constantly becomes the cause of suffering instead.

Actually, your job is merely a *condition* for your receiving a pay check. The principal cause of you getting paid is the good karma you created previously through giving generously to others or making offering to the Three Jewels of Refuge, other holy objects and so forth. It is also only through previously created good karma that you got your job in the first place—the job that itself is simply a condition for your getting paid.

Thus you can see that what you lack is education in how karma works.

All over the world you will find people who have never been educated at school or college or ever done a day's work in their lives but are extremely wealthy, possessing enough money to last several lifetimes. This shows that what is generally considered to be success—wealth and reputation—can be had without either outer education or what's called a "profession" or even a regular job. It all depends on karma.

ACTUAL PRACTICES FOR MAKING EACH MOMENT OF OUR LIVES MEANINGFUL

Working with bodhicitta

As you leave home for work, reflect on the meaning of your life— your universal responsibility to bring happiness to all sentient beings. If possible, generate bodhicitta consciously, by thinking, "In order to bring happiness to all sentient beings, I must achieve enlightenment, therefore, as a service to all beings, I am going to do my job."

If, for example, you're a secretary, think as you do your job that you are fulfilling others' wishes for happiness, that you are offering them happiness. If you are building a house, think that you are offering its future inhabitants, even the pets, the happiness of enjoying shelter, protection from the elements, heat and cold; helping them to have a long life. If you're a hairdresser, think that you are offering your clients the happiness of having the beautiful hair they want.

Whatever work you do, you can think in the same way. If you're a comedian, singer or musician, think that you are offering others the happiness of enjoying your performance, distracting them from sadness, depression or perhaps even anger.

Also, it is not enough simply to motivate with bodhicitta at the beginning of an action. As time passes, you have to check again and again to make sure that you are still working for others and not for your ego. If you find that you are motivated by the desire for your own happiness, you have to transform this negative attitude into bodhicitta again by remembering the kindness of other sentient beings, thinking, "I have received all my past, present and future happiness from other sentient beings; there is nothing more precious than them. The only thing to do in life is to work for their happiness; to do anything else is meaningless, empty. Even Buddha, Dharma and Sangha, my holy objects of refuge and prayer, come from sentient beings—how could anything be kinder or more precious than others?" Thus, every hour that you work with this attitude—feeling that others are extremely precious and wanting to benefit them in the highest way—becomes Dharma, the true cause of happiness, the cause of enlightenment.

Also, from time to time, rejoice. Fill your heart with happiness by thinking, "How fortunate I am that I can serve others completely, that I can offer them much happiness, that they can use me for their happiness."

Taking care of your child with bodhicitta

If you have clinging attachment for your child, everything you do to take care of him or her becomes the cause of samsara. Instead, think, "I am taking care of somebody who is the source of all my past, present and future happiness, all comfort and enjoyment, including the supreme happiness of enlightenment. Therefore, this child is a very precious person in my life, one of the numberless kind mother sentient beings. Moreover, this being's mind is obscured, under the control of delusion and karma and experiencing samsaric suffering, and completely dependent upon my help. Therefore, I am responsible to take care. Just as my own temporal and ultimate happiness depend on me, so do my child's."

This is the attitude with which you should take care of your children. From time to time, rejoice: "How wonderful it is. The purpose of my life is to serve all sentient beings, and here I have an opportunity to serve at least one of them completely. I am so fortunate that my body, speech and mind can be useful in bringing happiness to at least one sentient being."

This is how to make taking care of your children into a sincere Dharma practice. This way, even if you don't have time to do formal practice or retreat, you will never feel regret that you have completely wasted your life.

Otherwise, your reason for having children is the same as that for keeping a pet—your own comfort. The ordinary attitude is selfish pursuit of enjoyment for yourself alone, obsessively thinking, "This is my child; this child is mine," as if your children existed simply for your own use. You are motivated by clinging to the object and cherishing your I.

The most important education that you can give children is in ethics and the development of a good heart. Without this, they will have suffering lives, becoming, for example, unkind, violent, and disobedient, not only to others but also to the kind parents who provided them with a precious human body and took care of them in many other ways. Such children will have neither love nor compassion for others, and may even regard their parents as their worst enemy. Additionally, they can be easily influenced by wrong views and taught that these views are reality, for example, that their parents are responsible for all their problems. As a result, they can grow up hating their parents and regarding them as enemies. Because of their uncontrolled minds, such children's lives may fill with crime, relationship problems and depression, and instead of finding peace, satisfaction and fulfillment, they just feel that their lives are utterly without meaning.

The best way to be healthy and to avoid all sickness, even AIDS, is to have a good heart and pure ethics. This is also the best way to protect your life and live long. It enables sons and daughters to live in harmony with the rest of their family, especially their parents, and to be kind, loving and compassionate to all other people as well. At the very least, it reduces the suffering of relationships. Actually, whatever torture people experience is not inflicted by somebody else. It is caused by the person's own concepts of hatred, jealousy, dissatisfied desire and, especially, ignorance, the foundation of it all.

Ethics and a good heart make life much simpler, less complicated. If children are educated in this way, their lives will be peaceful, their hearts will be fulfilled and their deaths will be happy and controlled. Ethics prevent you from harming others, while a good heart makes you benefit them.

It is the responsibility of teachers and parents to give children this most important education of all. Moreover, parents and teachers themselves have to serve as both example and inspiration. Of course, they are limited in what they can do for a child by that child's individual karma. Therefore, everything that they wish for that child may not happen; the children themselves also have to make an effort. Nevertheless, parents and teachers are extremely important influences, and there is responsibility on both sides.

If children grow up with ethics and a good heart, they will not give harm to others, and as a result, others will love, support and not harm them.

Therefore, the way in which parents and teachers educate and influence children determines how much they harm or bring happiness to many other living beings. Your child can destroy the world or bring it peace and joy. And, of course, the way you bring up your children influences how they bring up their own.

Walking with bodhicitta

If you walk with bodhicitta, every step becomes the cause of the highest happiness, peerless enlightenment, for all sentient beings. Walk with strong awareness, thinking, "Each sentient being, each person, each insect, is the source of all my past, present and future happiness." This is called remembering sentient beings' "extensive" kindness. Reflecting on the four ways that all sentient beings have been kind to you as mother—giving you your precious human body, protecting you from harm, providing you with enjoyments and making sure that you receive a good education—is called awareness of their "numberless" kindness. As you walk with this awareness, whenever you see another sentient being, try to feel that being's kindness in particular. Whenever you practice these recollections, the conclusion that you should reach is the wish to free them from suffering and bring them all happiness; the wish to lead them all to enlightenment.

From the moment you leave home, practice mindfulness, keeping bodhicitta constantly in mind by thinking continuously, "The purpose of my life is to free all sentient beings from suffering and bring them happiness." Think like this with everybody you see—on the road, in shops, restaurants and cars, anybody you pass on foot and animals and insects everywhere. Walking back, again maintain constant awareness of bodhicitta until you get home.

This is the secret to enjoying life, to living a happy life in a meaningful way without allowing your ego to cheat you.

Walking with emptiness

You can also meditate on emptiness while you walk. This prevents your walking from becoming the cause of samsaric suffering in general and the unimaginable suffering of the three lower realms in particular. Instead, every step becomes a cure for the entire round of samsaric suffering and an antidote to the poisonous root of all delusions, ignorance—not perceiving that the I is empty from its own side. Meditating like this transforms your walking into the cause of liberation, freedom from samsara.

As you walk, ask yourself, "Why do I say, 'I'm walking'?" Analyze this. The only reason you can find for saying "I am walking" is the fact that your aggregate of body is performing the action called walking, that's all. Because your *skandha* of form is performing the action of walking, your mind comes up with the label "I am walking." Inside your body there appears to you an I that seems to exist from its own side. That's what you say is walking, but it's a complete hallucination; it doesn't exist at all. The I that you say is walking is merely imputed by your own mind. What appears to you and what you believe—a real, truly existent I that is not merely labeled by the mind—is a complete hallucination. It doesn't exist; it is empty.

You can apply this analysis to all other phenomena—roads, houses, trees, whatever. Just like the action of walking, they too are all merely labeled by your mind. What appears to be real, truly out there, is a hallucination. That is the object to be refuted.

Therefore, as you walk, be aware that in the sense that they all appear from their own side, I, action and object are all hallucinations. Then, no matter how long you walk, as long as you walk mindfully, it all becomes lam-rim, it all becomes a remedy to ignorance, a sword to cut the root of samsara, the root of all suffering.

Walking as if in a dream

Another simple way of meditating while you walk is to question yourself, "Does my I appear to be merely labeled or not?" It does not appear to be. "Does my action of walking appear to be merely labeled? Do the road, sky, cars, people, cats, dogs and ice-cream all appear to be merely labeled? Does whatever I see appear to be merely labeled by my mind or not?" No, all these things do not appear to you like that at all. Therefore, it is all like a dream, a hallucination. You are walking as if in a dream; the road, sky, cars, people and trees, your walking itself, are like a dream. (Even though I am saying this correctly, "like a dream," it is more effective for our minds to say that it "*is* a dream; I'm dreaming.")

Why meditate like this? When you practice mindfulness in this way, there is no clinging, no grasping, because you understand that everything is a hallucination, a dream, unreal. You realize that in fact, all those things that appear as something real coming from out there—a real I from out there, a real road from out there, a real sky from out there, real walking, real cars, real people, real trees, real enemies, real friends—are merely imputed by the mind. When you understand this, attachment and anger are less likely to arise. Thus, this practice brings peace to your mind immediately; your mind becomes detached and free, patient and without anger.

When you walk with the mindfulness that everything is a dream, you understand in your heart that everything is not real, does not exist. If you relate this understanding to the I, action and object, and so forth, that appear from there, you can see that they are empty. When you meditate that everything is like a dream, no matter what you see—the various shapes of people's bodies or the billions of other phenomena that you designate as ugly or beautiful—you know there is nothing to cling to, nothing to get angry at, because there is nothing to hold onto; in your heart you know that they don't exist. Seeing things in this way helps you to let go.

Therefore, just like the analytical meditation on emptiness while you walk, all the walking you do while meditating on everything as a dream also becomes a method to cut the root of samsara, a remedy to the entire cycle of samsaric suffering, including problems in your relationships, being treated badly by others and so forth. Walking with the mindfulness that everything is a dream eradicates delusion and karma, the fundamental cause of samsara, the main cause of suffering.

This is how to make walking the cause of ultimate happiness, complete liberation from samsara and its cause.

Walking with dependent arising

A fourth way of meditating while walking is to walk with

mindfulness of dependent arising. As I mentioned before, "I am walking because the aggregates are walking—my mind has simply fabricated the label, 'I am walking'"—in other words, the merely labeled I is merely labeled walking and merely labeled seeing the merely labeled sky, the merely labeled trees, the merely labeled people, the merely labeled beautiful man, the merely labeled beautiful woman, the merely labeled ugly buildings, the merely labeled cars, the merely labeled houses and so forth. This is walking with mindfulness of subtle dependent arising.

Walking with impermanence

You can also walk with meditation on impermanence and death. With every step you take, think how your life is running out, getting shorter and shorter. The faster you walk, the more aware of how quickly your life is finishing you become. Each step is bringing you closer to death and, if you fail to purify your negative karma, to the immeasurable suffering of the lower realms. (Similarly, when you're driving your car, feel like a condemned person being led to the gallows, each moment bringing you closer to your execution.)

This is how to practice the mindfulness of life finishing quickly, bringing you ever closer to death and the lower realms.

This meditation helps you deal with whatever problems you are facing right now—relationship problems, emotional problems, all your problems. Reflecting on impermanence and death puts an immediate end to desire, jealousy and anger. It quickly brings incredible peace to your mind and makes you more determined than ever to practice Dharma and not to waste your life. It encourages and inspires you to make everything you do a Dharma action. It is a very powerful meditation.

Eating with bodhicitta

Why should you offer your food and drink before you consume it? It's not because the buddhas are hungry. If you have taken refuge, of course, you have a commitment to offer all your food and drink, however, every time you offer your food and drink to the Guru Triple Gem, you create many causes of enlightenment. You are creating merit not only because you are making offerings to the Buddha. You are also making offerings to the Dharma and the Sangha, so your offering is that much more powerful. Furthermore, since you are making offerings to the Guru, you are creating the most extensive merit of all.

This practice comes from Guru Shakyamuni Buddha's compassion. By making it a refuge precept to offer all your food to the Triple Gem, Lord Buddha is making you create countless causes for inconceivable happiness every day, ensuring that you attain the peerless happiness of enlightenment—the complete eradication of all mistakes of mind and the achievement of all realizations—as soon as possible.

There is also another very important reason for offering all your food and drink to the Guru Triple Gem. The comfort and enjoyment you get from eating and drinking—your very life and health, your perfect human rebirth, your long life—all the benefits you experience every day, hour, minute and second, come from the kindness of other sentient beings, from even their mere existence; from their having endured unbearable suffering through being killed, tortured and harmed in other ways; from other people creating so much negative karma in growing food for you. This is what the food and drink you enjoy costs other sentient beings.

For example, there are visible and invisible sentient beings in the water you use for cooking and drinking. When the water is boiled, they all suffer. Think about the wheat you use for cakes, noodles or bread or the rice on which you base so many meals. In the West, the fields are plowed by machine, killing many small creatures such as insects, worms and mice. In the East, oxen are used to pull the plows, so not only do the tiny creatures suffer as before, but also these beasts of burden suffer greatly by having to work hard for long hours under the blazing sun. If land has to be cleared, the fires and bulldozing kill and injure many more sentient beings. Not only do farmers give sentient beings much harm and create much negative karma on our behalf, but they themselves also have to work long, hard hours preparing the fields, looking after the crops, harvesting the grain and getting it ready for sale.

Think how much suffering goes into each grain of rice you eat. Then think about the previous grain from which it came and the beginningless continuity of all those grains of rice. By thinking back carefully on the beginningless continuity of every grain of rice you eat, you can get a deep feeling for just how many sentient beings have suffered, created negative karma and been killed in order that you can eat. As a result, you'll no longer be able to bear eating food simply for your own benefit, happiness or enjoyment. It's the same with the vegetables and salad that you eat. Countless sentient beings have suffered by being harmed or killed in the ground or by having to harm or kill others by tilling the soil, poisoning worms and insects and so forth.

If you understand all this, there's no way you'll be able to eat simply for your own selfish enjoyment. You won't be able to stand doing that. You'll feel that you must make the food and drink you consume beneficial for others, especially those who have suffered so much in bringing it to you.

Therefore, first offer your food and drink to the Guru Triple Gem, and then dedicate the merits of this offering to those sentient beings who suffered so much on your behalf, as mentioned in the prayer below. By transforming each instance of eating and drinking into Dharma in this way, you create inconceivable merit, which becomes not only the cause of your own enlightenment, but by the way also brings you liberation from samsara, good rebirths and happiness in future lives, and, in the absence of clinging, happiness in this life too. And when you dedicate the merits of your offering to others, you bring all these different levels of happiness to all other sentient beings as well.

Food offering meditation

Generate bodhicitta motivation by thinking, "The purpose of my life is to free all sentient beings from suffering and lead them to happiness, especially the peerless happiness of full enlightenment. This universal responsibility is mine alone. In order to succeed in this, I must first attain full enlightenment myself. Therefore, I am going to practice the yoga of offering food and drink to the Guru Triple Gem."

Then reflect on the emptiness of yourself, the food, the action of offering, the merit field and the action of eating. Visualize first that the food you are offering becomes a vast ocean of nectar and the bowl it's in becomes a huge jeweled container. Now, multiply this and visualize numberless huge, jeweled containers filling all of space. Then recite the blessing mantra, which causes each buddha to receive numberless offerings:

OM NAMO BHAGAVATE VAJRA SARA PRAMARDINE TATHAGATAYA ARHATE SAMYAK SAMBUDDHAYA TAYATHA OM VAJRE VAJRE MAHAVAJRE MAHA TEJA VAJRE MAHA VIDYA VAJRE MAHA BODHICITTA VAJRE MAHA BODHI MANDO PASAM KRAMANA VAJRE SARVA KARMA AVARANA VISHODHANA VAJRE SOHA. (3x)

Then make the following offering prayers:

The guru is Buddha, the guru is Dharma,
The guru is Sangha also.
The guru is the source of all happiness—
I offer this food to all gurus.

In all future lives, may I and those around me
Never be separated from the Triple Gem,
Continuously make offerings to the Triple Gem,
And always receive the blessings of the Triple Gem.

The *Guru Puja* and other tantric practices explain that by making an offering to even one "pore" of the guru, which means, for example, one of the guru's pets, you accumulate more merit than you would by making that offering to all the buddhas of the past, present and future and the buddhas of the ten directions. Therefore, when it comes to creating extensive merit, there is no more powerful merit field than your virtuous friend. That's why Nagarjuna said, "Abandon all other offerings. Make offerings to only your guru. By pleasing him you will attain sublime wisdom, the state of omniscience."

If you can, elaborate on the method above by making offerings to the Triple Gem and all holy objects—statues, stupas, scriptures and so forth—in the ten directions, seeing them all as manifestations of your guru's holy mind, your offering generating infinite bliss in his holy mind.

Make charity of oceans of nectar to all sentient beings, fully satisfying each and every one. Dedicate the merit of this charity to their liberation and enlightenment.

Dedication

By generating bodhicitta, making offerings to your virtuous friend and the holy objects of the ten directions and making charity to all sentient beings, you have created infinite merit. Included in all sentient beings are the worms inside your body. Dedicate this infinite merit by praying, "Through the connection I have established by making charity to all 21,000 microscopic worms inside my body, may they be reborn human in their very next life and may I be able to guide them to enlightenment by showing them the Dharma in all future lives.

"Because of these merits, may I, my entire family, all Dharma students and all other sentient beings in all future lifetimes never be separated from the Triple Gem, always make offerings to the Triple Gem, and receive the blessings of the Triple Gem. May I, the other students and all other sentient beings, especially the benefactors of this food and all those who worked, suffered and died in bringing it to me, quickly realize the entire Dharma path, from guru devotion up to enlightenment without even a second's delay.

"Because of the past, present and future merit created by myself, the buddhas and bodhisattvas and all other sentient beings, which is empty from its own side, may the I, which is empty from its own side, attain Guru Shakyamuni's enlightenment, which is empty from its own side, and lead all sentient beings, who are empty from their own side, to that enlightened state, which is empty from its own side, as quickly as possible, by myself alone."

Further explanation of this practice

Whether or not you know any offering prayers, the most important meditation you can do is that on the emptiness of yourself, the food and the action of eating. Also, visualize that you are not offering ordinary food but a vast ocean of nectar, which pleases all the buddhas. Offer it to the Buddha, Dharma and Sangha and all the holy objects of the ten directions—statues, stupas, scriptures and so forth. If you also visualize that these holy objects are manifestations of your root guru, because of the enormous power of the object, the guru with whom you've established a Dharma relationship, you accumulate the greatest possible merit. Then you make charity of the food to all sentient beings, visualizing that they all become enlightened as a result.

To do this practice, you can visualize the *Guru Puja* merit field and all the virtuous friends with whom you have a connection, seeing them all as emanations of your root guru. Then you make the offering. This is the elaborate meditation; you can also do an abbreviated one.

It is said in the teachings that during your lifetime, 21,000 tiny worms live in your body. Pray, "Through this connection, I shall teach them Dharma in all future lives and lead them to enlightenment."

By meditating like this you create infinite merit in five different ways: by generating bodhicitta motivation; by making offerings to your gurus; by making offerings to the Triple Gem; by making offerings to all the other holy objects; and by making offerings to all sentient beings. The more merit you accumulate, the closer you get to enlightenment. The closer you get to enlightenment, the closer you get to bringing all sentient beings to enlightenment.

Finally, dedicate the merit to be able to actualize the entire lam-rim in your own mind and in the minds of all other sentient beings, especially in the minds of your family members and any people who are sick or dying that you specifically want to remember in your prayers. Seal your dedication to achieve enlightenment for the sake of all sentient beings by meditating on emptiness, as above. Then, eat as mindfully as possible.

If you have received a highest yoga tantra initiation, while making the offering, stabilize your concentration of yourself as the deity, maintaining constant awareness that wherever the deity is, there too is your guru—you, the deity and your guru are one. With each mouthful of food or drink, remain mindful that you are offering it to your guru-deity. If you maintain the clear appearance of your body in the aspect of the holy body of the deity, you are practicing what is known in tantra as pure appearance and pure divine pride, and each mouthful becomes a tsog offering. Since you are making this offering to your guru, you accumulate the greatest possible merit. Finally, since this meditation is a part of your samaya to visualize yourself as the deity, you are fulfilling your commitment to do so.

If you have not received a great initiation, visualize in your heart Guru Shakyamuni Buddha or a deity with whom you feel a close connection or to whom you pray, such as Tara or Chenrezig.

If, while making the offering, you concentrate on the Buddha or the deity at your heart as inseparably one with your guru, your practice becomes a form of guru yoga, like that in the *Guru Puja* or the *Six Session Yoga* or other guru yoga practices that you might have heard of.

Shopping with bodhicitta

When you go shopping, if you buy something for someone else, think sincerely of the other person's happiness and offer the gift without attachment clinging to your own happiness. If you are buying something for your own use, think, "I'm the servant of all sentient beings. My job is to free them from all suffering and lead them to enlightenment. Therefore, even though I am using this object, ultimately, it is for them." This is the way to use the things you buy—with the thought that you are the servant of others and that whatever you enjoy is ultimately for them.

If you shop with bodhicitta, not only do you avoid creating negative karma, but you also create the cause of supreme enlightenment for yourself and all sentient beings. If you shop with renunciation, you create the cause of happiness. If you shop with meditation on emptiness, by cutting the root of ignorance, you create the cause of liberation from samsara. Shopping with bodhicitta is best, because it brings you to enlightenment.

Partying with bodhicitta

When you give a party, think, "I am responsible for the happiness of all sentient beings. The purpose of my life is to free all sentient beings from suffering and lead them to all happiness, especially the peerless happiness of full enlightenment. This is my universal responsibility. To succeed in this I must first reach enlightenment myself, therefore I am going to do the Dharma practice of offering food and drink to others."

If you throw a party for only your own happiness, with ego and attachment, the evil thought of the eight worldly dharmas, clinging to the comfort of this life, your motivation is completely negative and the entire event becomes completely non-virtuous. No matter how many thousands of guests you entertain, all you do is create negative karma, countless causes for rebirth in the lower realms. If, however, your motivation for having a party and offering food and drink to others is a Dharma motivation from one of the three levels of virtue, it all becomes the cause of happiness.

Not only when you're giving a party, but even when you offer food and drink to others in the course of normal daily life, if you visualize them as manifestations of your guru and think that you are making an offering to him, you accumulate the most extensive merit. If you visualize the people to whom you are offering the food and drink as the deity to whom you pray, you are practicing tantra and creating unbelievable merit, much more than you would with simple charity. In this way, even if you give a person something quite small, like a glass of water or a piece of candy, you have made an incredibly successful business transaction, the result of which is unceasing happiness. Furthermore, if you and the person to whom you are giving the water or candy are both disciples of the same guru and you remember him at that time, the merit you create is greater than that of making offerings to the numberless buddhas of the three times and the ten directions.

Thus, everything becomes the cause of enlightenment; you have made the greatest possible profit out of that. No matter how little money you spent, the end result is not only enlightenment and, of course, all the other happinesses that lead up to it, but also you have avoided creating negative karma, the cause of samsara and the lower realms.

Going to the toilet with bodhicitta

Even going to the toilet can be made useful for yourself and others. Visualize above the crown of your head your guru and Vajrasattva, the powerful deity of purification, as one. Visualize all sentient beings at your heart. From Vajrasattva, nectar rushes down through the crown of your head to the sentient beings at your heart, purifying them of all their diseases, negative karma, obscurations and spirit harm. Recite either the short or the long Vajrasattva mantras. While doing so, visualize that whatever you excrete is actually all the sentient beings' diseases, in the form of pus and blood; negative karma and obscurations, in the form of filthy black liquid; and spirit harm, in the form of snakes, frogs and the like.

You can also visualize the opening of the toilet as the mouth of the Lord of Death, and as all the negativity enters, it turns into nectar. When you have finished, imagine that the Lord of Death's mouth closes and is sealed by a vajra, and you and all other sentient beings are purified. This meditation also helps you enjoy a long and healthy life. Finally, the Lord of Death sinks hundreds of feet deep into the ground, from where it is impossible to return.

Lama Yeshe once observed that in New York City, the best place to retreat is in the toilet! He might have said this because he used to give so much of his time to others—talking with people, spending time with their families and children—that perhaps it was only when he went to the bathroom that he found time to do his meditation practices.

If you do this toilet yoga, you get to do your Vajrasattva practice several times a day. This can only help you, as in this way, any negative karma that you have created and any broken precepts or damaged commitments get purified soon, before they've had much time to multiply. Going to the toilet offers you this incredible opportunity.

Short Vajrasattva mantra
OM VAJRASATTVA HUM

Long Vajrasattva mantra
OM VAJRASATTVA SAMAYA MANUPALAYA, VAJRASATTVA DENOPA TITHA, DIDO ME BHAVA, SUTO KAYO ME BHAVA, SUPO KAYO ME BHAVA, ANURAKTO ME BHAVA, SARVA SIDDHI ME PRAYATSA, SARVA KARMA SU TSAME, TSITTAM SHRIYAM KURU HUM, HA HA HA HA HO, BHAGAVAN SARVA TATHAGATA, VAJRA MAME MUNTSA, VAJRA BHAVA MAHA SAMAYA SATTVA AH HUM PHET

The meaning of the mantra: You, Vajrasattva, have generated the holy mind [bodhicitta] according to your pledge [samaya]. Your holy mind is enriched with the simultaneous holy actions of releasing transmigratory beings from samsara [the circling, suffering aggregates]. Whatever happens in my life—happiness or suffering, good or bad—with a pleased, holy mind, never give up but please guide me. Please stabilize all happiness, including the happiness of the upper realms, actualize all actions and sublime and common realizations, and please make the glory of the five wisdoms abide in my heart.

Sleeping with bodhicitta

There are many different kinds of meditation you can do before going to sleep. There are the profound meditations of tantra, but generally, you can generate the motivation of bodhicitta by thinking, "The purpose of my life is to free all sentient beings from suffering and lead them to happiness, especially the peerless happiness of enlightenment. I have this universal responsibility. To succeed in this, I must first attain enlightenment myself, therefore, I am going to practice the yoga of sleeping." With this bodhicitta motivation, go to sleep.

Another common meditation is to visualize your guru on your pillow, and when you lie down, your head rests in his lap. Then, in the presence of your guru, who with devotion you visualize as one with the buddha, generate compassion for all sentient beings and go to sleep. If you do this, your entire night's sleep will be virtuous, the cause of happiness. Thus, you can go to bed with devotion to your guru, with devotion to the buddha and with compassion for all sentient beings by reflecting on their suffering.

You can also think that as you go to sleep you are in the pure land of the deity you practice. This leaves positive imprints on your mind and you create the karma to be reborn in that pure land when you die.

You can also go to sleep with the thought of renunciation, reflecting on the suffering nature of samsara, impermanence and death and so forth, or by meditating on emptiness or dependent arising, looking at everything as a dream or an illusion, as merely labeled by the mind. If you go to bed mindful that everything that appears to you as not merely labeled by the mind is a dream, an hallucination, it can help you recognize your dreams as dreams and to practice virtue while you are dreaming. No matter which of these techniques you practice, your sleep becomes Dharma, virtue.

In tantra, there are two sleeping yogas: that of conventional truth and that of absolute truth. If you have received a great initiation, you can learn the details of these practices from the commentaries on the practice of that deity.

In the lam-rim there's some advice on how to get up early in the morning without being overwhelmed by sleep. Before getting into bed the night before, wash your feet while thinking of light. Try it; it works.

As I mentioned above, you can also go to sleep visualizing whichever pure land in which you'd like to be reborn. This can also help should you die suddenly. If you have trained your mind in this practice and generated the strong wish to be reborn in that pure land, during the death process you may be able to direct your consciousness to be reborn there.

Experiencing illness and death with bodhicitta

The very heart of Dharma practice, the best of all, the ultimate thought transformation, the supreme psychology, is to experience your problems on behalf of others.

Perhaps you have AIDS or cancer. Maybe you're having problems in your relationship or suffering from depression. Possibly you're dying. Whatever trouble you're experiencing, think, "I'm experiencing this problem on behalf of all sentient beings, to bring them happiness. I am taking on the AIDS [or cancer, relationship problems, depression, whatever] of all those who are suffering from AIDS at the moment and for all those who have the karma to get it. I take it all upon myself. I am experiencing this disease on behalf of all sentient beings who either have it or will get it." No matter what has happened to you—asthma, depression, business failure, being raped—you can dedicate it in the same way.

Throughout the day, as soon as the thought "I have AIDS" arises, immediately think, "I am experiencing this for the sake of all sentient beings."

When you are dying, think, "I am experiencing death for the numberless sentient beings who are also experiencing the suffering of dying at this very moment. I take it all upon myself. May they be free from the suffering of death and receive ultimate happiness right now." Try to die with this thought.

Each time you think this way, you purify unbelievable eons of negative karma and create merit as limitless as the sky. Each time you practice taking the suffering of others upon yourself, you come much closer to enlightenment, which means you come much closer to bringing all sentient beings to enlightenment. There is no more beneficial way to die than to die with this bodhicitta thought.

His Holiness the Dalai Lama calls people who can die like this completely self-supporting, because through familiarity with the various death meditations, at the most critical time of their lives, death, they can guide themselves skillfully to the next life.

Conclusion

If twenty-four hours a day, everything you do is motivated by bodhicitta, you accumulate infinite merit. Moreover, every single action becomes a cause for not only your own enlightenment but also the happiness of every other sentient being.

This is the way to make your life both as meaningful and as rich as possible.

THREE

A Daily Practice to Stop All Suffering
The Bodhisattva's Confession of Moral Downfalls

To put an end to our samsaric suffering, we must do two things. One is to purify the negative actions that we've done every day of our lives and the negativities we've created since beginningless time in our infinite previous lives as well. But that alone is not enough. We also have to change our minds and our actions and abstain from creating further negativities. If we don't, there'll be no end to our having to purify. If we don't change our minds and our actions, if we don't stop creating negative karma, there will always be more negativity to purify. Practicing purification with the four opponent powers can help us both purify negative karma already created and not create more.

To avoid experiencing the suffering results of negative karma, especially rebirth in the lower realms as well as the suffering experienced in the human and deva realms, we should engage in powerful purification practices, such as Vajrasattva meditation, confession before the Thirty-five Buddhas and the various other purification practices. Here I would like to explain briefly how to apply these in everyday life, with emphasis on prostrations to the Thirty-five Buddhas [see Appendix 3].

The moment you get up in the morning, generate bodhicitta

motivation. Determine to make the best use of your life by making it beneficial for other sentient beings. In other words, make the strong determination to live your life with bodhicitta all the time. Start by rejoicing that you are still alive, that you didn't die during the night but were born again today as a human being with the opportunity to practice Dharma, to achieve any of the three great meanings—the happiness of future lives, the happiness of liberation from samsara and the peerless happiness of full enlightenment. In every moment of this life, you can create the cause of any of these happinesses you wish.

Make the strong determination that from now on, especially in this life, especially during this day, you will never separate from bodhicitta, not even for a minute or a second, and will never allow yourself to fall under the influence of the self-cherishing thought. "I will never allow myself to be controlled by the self-cherishing thought." If you don't make this strong determination, you won't be able to practice bodhicitta, compassion for others. "I will not allow myself to be controlled by the self-cherishing thought, especially in this life, especially today, not for a minute or even a second." Make that kind of strong determination.

Basically, this should be your attitude towards the whole of your life, as explained in the teaching on a lifetime's practice integrated with the five powers. [See *Liberation in the Palm of Your Hand*, pp. 612-16 and *Advice From a Spiritual Friend*, pp. 111-12. The five powers are the power of the white seed, the power of familiarity, the power of determination, the power of repudiation and the power of prayer.] Even if you don't know many prayers, many different practices, if you can practice these five powers, you are doing the most important practice there is. Even if you aren't familiar with many Dharma teachings or texts, if you know what the five powers are and live your life accordingly, you give yourself much freedom, peace and happiness and can achieve enlightenment quickly. That's the greatest advantage, the greatest benefit.

After generating your morning motivation, do prostrations to the Thirty-five Buddhas. I am going to give you a few details of the meditation that is done with this practice so that you'll be able to create more merit when you do it. The more meditation skills you have, the more extensive the merit you create, the sooner you gain realizations and the closer you and all sentient beings come to enlightenment. If you have the skills, you can collect extensive skies of merit with every prostration that you do.

MOTIVATION

Before you start the actual practice, you should generate a strong feeling for wanting to purify by thinking along these lines: "The purpose of my life is to free all sentient beings from all their suffering and bring them to full enlightenment. To do this, I myself must first achieve enlightenment, so I must actualize the steps of the path to enlightenment. Therefore, I need to purify all my defilements, negative karmas and downfalls."

Generate regret. First recall the definition of negative karma—any action that results in suffering, usually an action motivated by ignorance, attachment or aversion—and think, "Almost every action I do, twenty-four hours a day, is motivated by worldly concern, attachment to the comfort of this life. It is like this from birth to death in this life and has been like that from beginningless rebirths. Nearly every action I have ever created has been non-virtuous, the cause of suffering. Not only that, but continuously I have also been breaking my pratimoksha, bodhisattva and tantric vows. Worst of all, I have created the heaviest of negative karmas in relation to my virtuous friends—getting angry at them, not believing what they say, having non-devotional thoughts towards them, harming their holy body and disobeying their advice. Having these negative imprints on my mental continuum is unbearable. It's as if I've swallowed a lethal poison. I must practice the antidote right away and purify all this negative karma immediately, without a second's delay."

Think of the lower realms, of the hell realms. "If I were now in a hell realm, how would it be? I would be totally overwhelmed by suffering, by the heaviest suffering of samsara. I would have no freedom to practice Dharma."

Then think, "Even though I'm not dead yet, my death could happen at any moment. At any moment, I could be there in the most terrifying hell realm, the unbearable suffering state. Therefore, without even a second's delay, I must purify all my defilements, all my negative karmas, all my downfalls. Therefore, I'm going to do prostrations with the meditation-recitation of the Thirty-five Buddhas, *The Confession of Downfalls*, to cause all sentient beings to receive all happiness up to that of enlightenment; in other words, to benefit all sentient beings."

With such thoughts, generate a strong feeling of urgency and regret. Your attitude should be one of wishing to purify yourself, but at the end, expand your attitude to include others with the wish to benefit all sentient beings by bringing them all happiness up to that of enlightenment. With the strong wish to purify yourself in order to benefit others, you then do the prostrations. Even if you do just a few prostrations, if they are done with this strong thought of purifying yourself in order to benefit others, each prostration and recitation of each of the Thirty-five Buddhas' names becomes extremely powerful.

The importance of memorizing the names of the Thirty-five Buddhas

If you are doing this practice in a group and one person leads the chanting while the others do not recite the names of the Thirty-five Buddhas because they have not memorized them, only one person gets the benefit of the recitation. Those who haven't memorized the names will get the benefits of making prostrations, but they won't get the benefit of reciting the names. This is a great loss. How? Take the very first name, that of Guru Shakyamuni Buddha, for example. By reciting Guru Shakyamuni Buddha's name, you purify 80,000 eons of negative karma; if you don't recite his name, this doesn't happen. Reciting each of the Thirty-five Buddhas' names purifies a certain number of eons of negative karma or a particular negative karma. Reciting each name just one time purifies many eons of negative karma.

If someone told you that you would not get cancer for six eons, you would think that that was fantastic. Forget about the six eons, even if someone told you that you would not get cancer in this life, you would think it fantastic, unbelievably good fortune. Now here, in relation to the practice of the Thirty-five Buddhas, we are talking about your not getting cancer or any other problem for thousands of eons because you have purified that many eons of negative karma, which is the cause of not only sickness but that of all other problems and obstacles. Cancer is just a tiny drop in the ocean of samsaric suffering. Purifying even two thousand eons of negative karma is incredibly advantageous. If you were going to die right now, in the next moment, the most important thing, the most urgent thing, you could do would be to purify your negative karma.

If you were about to die, which would you prefer to be given: a billion dollars or the chance to purify this life's negative karma? Which is more important? Which is more precious? Of course, purifying even one negative karma before you die is much better than receiving a billion or even a trillion dollars.

My point is that if only one person recites the names of the Thirty-five Buddhas, only that person receives the advantage of all this purification. Those who don't recite the names don't receive the benefit. It's like one person trying to eat a meal on behalf of a group of people while they don't eat. The food that person eats doesn't fill the other people's stomachs, doesn't satisfy their hunger.

The great advantage of having memorized the names of the Thirty-five Buddhas is that you can recite them in the car or train while going to work. Since you spend so much time going back and forth between home and work, it is good to spend that time doing prayers or reciting the names of the Thirty-five Buddhas. You can also recite them when you are flying by plane. It's all right to read them from a book, but it is much easier if you know the names by heart, because then you can purify at any time. Since reciting these buddhas' names even once purifies many eons of negative karma, it's a great loss if you don't recite them. It will take you longer to purify your negative karma and gain realizations, and longer to achieve enlightenment, which means that the numberless other sentient beings who are karmically connected to you will have to experience more suffering.

Therefore, you must realize what a precious opportunity you have right now. This present time is the most precious time. If you don't take this opportunity to practice, it is a great loss. There is no greater loss than this; it's a greater loss than losing a million dollars, zillions of dollars. Some people, when their business collapses or they lose a million dollars, become crazy and want to jump off a bridge or the roof of a building. Such losses are nothing, just something material, meaningless. But here, if you don't take the incredible opportunity to practice confession with the Thirty-five Buddhas, to purify your negative karma and collect merit in such an easy way, you have suffered the greatest loss.

Even if you owned skies of diamonds, gold or wish-fulfilling gems, that alone could not purify your negative karma or stop you from being reborn in the lower realms. However, even if you don't own any of this wealth, if you recite Guru Shakyamuni Buddha's name just once, you purify 80,000 eons of negative karma.

Reciting the name of any of the Thirty-five Buddhas purifies many thousands of eons of negative karma. Even if you were to lose that much wealth, it would be nothing compared to losing the chance of practicing the Thirty-five Buddhas. This is such an easy way to purify and to collect extensive merit. Simply by reciting the names of the Thirty-five Buddhas, you can achieve unbelievable purification.

THE SEVEN MEDICINE BUDDHAS

After reciting the names of the Thirty-five Buddhas, you recite the names of the seven Medicine Buddhas, who are extremely powerful not only for healing but for success in general. This is because when those seven buddhas were bodhisattvas they prayed and dedicated for sentient beings to be able to overcome their problems and achieve all success. Therefore, praying to the Medicine Buddhas and reciting their names is an extremely precious practice and is very effective for both healing and success. Those who recite the seven Medicine Buddhas' names and the Medicine Buddha mantra in their daily lives will never be reborn in the lower realms and, no matter what happens, will have no fear of death. Any human being or animal who at the time of death simply hears the name or mantra of the Medicine Buddha will also not be reborn in the lower realms. This practice is very important. Kachen Yeshe Gyaltsen and other recent lineage lamas recited the names of the seven Medicine Buddhas right after reciting the names of the Thirty-five Buddhas. This addition makes this powerful purification practice even more powerful.

HOW TO DO PROSTRATIONS TO THE THIRTY-FIVE BUDDHAS AND THE SEVEN MEDICINE BUDDHAS

When you recite these buddhas' names, it would be extremely beneficial if you could do three sets as a daily practice. That means you could be doing as many as 150 prostrations each session, depending on how many you make during the confession prayer. Also, if you have room, you should always do full-length prostrations. You create unbelievably extensive merit if you do. Cover as much ground with your body as you possibly can; when you go down, make your body as long as you can.

Start by doing three prostrations with the mantra OM NAMO MANJUSHRIYE.... Then, in English or Tibetan, recite the refuge formula. If you do it in Tibetan, make prostrations while reciting *Lama-la kyab su chi wo* (I take refuge in the Guru) as many times as you can during one prostration. Then, when your forehead touches the ground, change to *Sangye-la kyab su chi wo* (I take refuge in the Buddha), and keep reciting that until, on your next prostration, your forehead touches the ground again. Then change to *Chö-la kyab su chi wo* (I take refuge in the Dharma) and keep prostrating through *Gendun-la kyab su chi wo* (I take refuge in the Sangha).

Then, when you next touch the ground with your forehead, change to *Tön-pa chom-dän-dä de-zhin-sheg-pa*...(Guru Shakyamuni Buddha's name). If you have memorized it, you should recite it as fast as you can. It's unbelievable—each repetition purifies 80,000 eons of negative karma. That's why you should memorize all of the Thirty-five Buddhas' names. The more times you recite each one, the better.

When you do business, you try to maximize your profits. You try to get as many dollars as you can from each transaction. It's the same here, except that with reciting the buddhas' names, the profits are so much greater. Reciting just one buddha's name is much more profitable than billions of dollars of business profit. As I have been saying, reciting the name of just one of the Thirty-five Buddhas, not even all thirty-five, purifies many thousands of eons of negative karma. The merit you collect in this way is much more profitable than billions of dollars. Which is more profitable—making a billion dollars or reciting one buddha's name just once? There's no comparison. A billion dollars is worth nothing compared to that. No amount of money can purify many eons of negative karma or generate extensive merit, but reciting a buddha's name can.

After your forehead touches the ground, change to the next buddha's name and recite it as fast and as many times as you can. Keep going through all their names until you have recited all thirty-five. I recite the last one three times. Why? Not because other people do but because the thirty-fifth buddha's name, *De-zhin-sheg-pa...wang-gyi gyäl-po* (*Tathagata, arhat, perfectly completed enlightened one, King of the Lord of Mountains, Firmly seated on Jewel and Lotus*), purifies broken samayas and negative karma created in relation to your gurus, which are the heaviest negative karmas of all. Therefore, I think it's necessary to recite the last buddha's name three times.

By then adding the names of the seven Medicine Buddhas, all your prayers—for special realizations from your Dharma practice, for good things to happen to you, for the benefit of others—will be successful. Your own prayers will be successful and you will also receive the beneficial effects of all the prayers made by the seven Medicine Buddhas in the past. Therefore, it is very important to recite the names of the Medicine Buddhas in addition to those of the Thirty-five Buddhas. Again recite each name as many times as possible during each prostration. However, you only need to recite the seven Medicine Buddhas' names once each session—after the first repetition of the Thirty-five Buddhas. You don't need to do them the second or third time.

If you recite them a second or third time, in the first set, recite the Thirty-five Buddhas and the seven Medicine Buddhas, then go back to the refuge for the second time. After the second set of Thirty-five Buddhas, go back to the refuge again, like that. Three sets. If you can make this your regular practice it would be extremely, unbelievably good. If three sets are not possible, do two. If not two, then one. But remember, with each prostration, recite that buddha's name as many times as you can, over and over, rather than reciting it slowly throughout the prostration, just once. Each day that you recite the names of the Thirty-five Buddhas—each day that you recite just one buddha's name—makes your life very different, like the difference between earth and sky. Your mind carries much less negative karma, and that which it does carry is much lighter. Your life will be much more successful, especially in attaining realizations, and you will be able to benefit others much more in both this and future lives.

THE VISUALIZATION AND THE ABSOLUTE GURU

When you visualize Guru Shakyamuni Buddha, visualize Avalokiteshvara at his heart. The psychology of this was explained by the great yogi Sangye Yeshe, who said, "Without the guru, there is no buddha," which means that all buddhas come from the guru.

At the heart of the explanation of guru yoga lies the dharmakaya. In general, we can call this omniscient mind, but to be specific we should call it the extremely subtle mind of the wisdom of great bliss non-dual with the emptiness of all existence. "Non-dual" means the wisdom that sees the emptiness of all existence directly—not from afar, like when we look at distant things, but through having thoroughly pervaded all phenomena— the wisdom of great bliss seeing all emptiness directly and non-dualistically, like water mixed with water, through having completely eradicated the dualistic view. This is dharmakaya; this is what is called the absolute guru.

When we talk about the guru we can refer to either the absolute or the conventional guru. But even if the absolute guru manifested right now in the aspect of the Buddha, we wouldn't be able to see him because our minds are obscured. Therefore, the only way in which the absolute guru can communicate with us is by manifesting in an ordinary human body, a form with samsaric suffering, delusions and mistaken actions. It is only by taking this imperfect form that the absolute guru can communicate with us, manifesting in an ordinary mistaken aspect according to our impure, obscured, mistaken mind; this ordinary aspect is all we can see with our present state of mind.

Thus, the only way the absolute guru can guide us, especially when it comes to giving teachings, is through this ordinary, mistaken, human form. We don't have the karma to see an aspect purer than this. Even if the guru were to manifest in a pure form, we couldn't see it. On the other hand, if the absolute guru manifested in a lower form, like that of an animal, that too would be difficult for us to recognize, and it would also be hard to communicate through such a form, to give teachings and so forth. Therefore, this ordinary aspect, which shows delusion and suffering, is very precious, very important, because it is through manifesting in this form that all the buddhas guide us.

If we can understand this, we will realize just how kind the guru is. In this human aspect, the guru grants us the three vows—pratimoksha, bodhisattva and tantric—leading us to happiness in future lives, better rebirths, freedom from samsara and, ultimately, highest enlightenment, cessation of the two levels of obscuration, gross and subtle, and completion of all realizations.

In Tibet and neighboring countries, even the person who taught you the alphabet was regarded as a guru. The only reason people learned the alphabet was so that they could study Dharma, and that was also why the teacher taught it. It was quite different from ordinary school.

Therefore, we refer to the person who teaches the alphabet,

who gives oral transmissions of and commentaries on the sutras, and who gives initiations and explanations, commentaries and meditation instructions on tantra—freeing us from all samsaric suffering and obscurations and leading us to enlightenment in these various ways—as the conventional guru. This is the dharmakaya, the absolute guru, guiding us to enlightenment by revealing the entire path through the ordinary mistaken form we call the conventional guru. This happens not so much because of the omniscient mind and perfect power of the absolute guru, the dharmakaya, the transcendent wisdom of non-dual bliss and void, but because the absolute guru is bound by infinite compassion that encompasses us and all other sentient beings, without a single exception. This infinite compassion compels the dharmakaya to manifest in numberless different forms according to the minds of sentient beings, leading us to enlightenment gradually—from life to life, from happiness to happiness.

Therefore, whenever we say "Guru Shakyamuni Buddha," we should remember that "Guru" refers to the absolute guru, who guides us by manifesting in the ordinary form of the conventional guru. Guru Shakyamuni Buddha is the absolute guru manifesting as Shakyamuni Buddha to guide us to enlightenment. Therefore, "Guru Shakyamuni Buddha" implies the oneness of the absolute and conventional gurus, and the mind that sees this oneness is the mind of guru yoga. Previously, you saw the Buddha and the guru as separate; that mind was not the guru yoga mind. When you see them with devotion as one, you have transformed your mind into the guru yoga mind.

Why do we visualize the Compassionate Buddha Avalo-kiteshvara at the heart of Shakyamuni Buddha? The Thirty-five Buddhas who transform from the heart of Shakyamuni Buddha do so out of compassion, in order to purify us, so we visualize compassion at the heart of Shakyamuni Buddha to signify this.

Guru Shakyamuni Buddha, at the center of the visualization, is the first of the Thirty-five Buddhas, the rest of whom are in the aspect of the five *Dhyani* Buddhas. Beams emanate from Avalokiteshvara at the heart of Guru Shakyamuni Buddha. At the end of each beam is a throne supported by a white elephant adorned with pearls, and on each throne is seated one of the remaining thirty-four buddhas. The first six are in the aspect of Akshobhya and are blue in color, with the exception of the Naga King, whose body is blue and head is white. They are seated, showing the same earth-touching mudra as Guru Shakyamuni Buddha.

The next seven are white in color and in the aspect of Vairo-chana. The next seven are yellow in color and in the aspect of Ratnasambhava. The next seven are red in color and in the aspect of Amitabha. The next seven are green in color and in the aspect of Amoghasiddhi. Their postures are those of the respective Dhyani Buddha.

Visualizing elephants supporting the thrones makes the purification more powerful. Adorning them with pearls makes it even stronger.

There are many different ways of visualizing the Thirty-five Buddhas, in accordance with the various traditions of this practice. For example, there is the way Lama Tsong Khapa did it when he made hundreds of thousands of prostrations to the Thirty-five Buddhas in his cave at Wölka, in Tibet. The simplest way to do it is as above, dividing the Thirty-five Buddhas into five groups of seven and visualizing them in the aspect of the Five Dhyani buddhas.

Before you start prostrating, take refuge in Guru, Buddha, Dharma and Sangha. Then, as you start to prostrate, recite the names of the Thirty-five Buddhas one by one. As you recite the name of Guru Shakyamuni Buddha, you prostrate to all Thirty-five Buddhas, but especially to Guru Shakyamuni Buddha. As you recite the name of the second buddha, you again prostrate to all, but especially to that one. Repeat this as you complete the recitation of all Thirty-five Buddhas' names.

Lama Atisha once explained why this practice is so powerful. When these buddhas were bodhisattvas following the Mahayana path to enlightenment, they made many prayers and dedications, such as, "When I become enlightened, may the negative karma of anybody who prays or prostrates to me be completely purified." Because of the power of these prayers, made with compassion for the benefit of others, even one repetition of these buddhas' names purifies a vast amount of negative karma. Buddhas have many qualities, one of which is the power of prayer, or aspiration. This power ensures that whatever prayers that buddha made in the past are realized. Therefore, we benefit from the prayers made for sentient beings' purification by the Thirty-five Buddhas.

PURIFICATION BEFORE GOING TO BED

Every night, before going to bed, do Vajrasattva practice, reciting one mala, a half mala, or at least twenty-one repetitions of the long mantra. If you can combine your recitation with prostrations, it will be very, very powerful; two powerful practices combined. You will collect extensive merit and purify unbelievably heavy negative karma. Otherwise, you can do your Vajrasattva recitation while seated. It depends on whether or not you have the opportunity to do prostrations and on how you feel. You can decide for yourself.

And if you can begin your evening Vajrasattva practice with prostrations to the Thirty-five Buddhas, going straight through and not necessarily repeating each buddha's name over and over with each prostration as in the morning practice described above, that will also be very powerful because, as I have said, reciting each buddha's name even *once* purifies many thousands of eons of negative karma. This practice is unbelievably powerful.

THE BENEFITS OF PROSTRATIONS

By doing prostrations, you purify obscurations and receive the enlightened qualities of the holy body, speech and mind of a buddha. Even putting your hands together at your heart is a prostration. The sutras explain that making even this simple gesture to a holy object has eight benefits:

1. In future lives you will receive a good body with perfect shape, organs and senses.

2. You will receive perfect conditions so that your practice will be successful and your wishes fulfilled, and you will be able to work for the teachings and sentient beings.

3. You will be able to live in morality. (Without morality, there is no happiness in future lives, liberation or enlightenment.)

4. You will have devotion. (Without devotion, there are no realizations.)

5. You will have a courageous mind. (Without a courageous mind you cannot continue to practice Dharma or do extensive bodhisattva work for the teachings and sentient beings.)

6. You will be reborn as a deva or a human being.

7. You will achieve the arya path.

8. You will achieve enlightenment.

Whenever you go into a temple, remember that even a simple prostration to just one Buddha statue has these eight benefits. However, in a single temple there may be hundreds of statues and paintings of the Buddha, so prostrating like this to each one as you look at them is unbelievably beneficial. In addition to the merit you create by circumambulating temples and stupas, it is good to use your hands to accumulate merit by making simple prostrations in this way. Since prostrating to even one holy object creates great merit, this is an easy way for you to accumulate extensive merit.

It is said that holy objects are manifestations of the Buddha. Even though we don't have the karma to see the actual living Buddha, by appearing as statues, stupas, scriptures and other holy objects, the Buddha allows us to accumulate merit. Some sentient beings can see these manifestations of the Buddha, others cannot. In Tibet there were people who were unable to see the Guru Shakyamuni Buddha statue in the Jokhang Temple, Lhasa's holiest shrine. To them, the temple appeared to be completely dark; they couldn't see anything. After much purification, one person who had this problem was eventually able to see the light of the butter-lamps but he still could not see the statue. Another person saw only piles of dried meat on the thrones instead of the statues. Just because the statues are there does not mean that everybody can see them. It depends on one's level of the mind.

The teachings say that animals cannot see holy objects. At Kopan I lift the dogs up to show them the thangkas, but I don't think that they see what we do. It may be very rare for an animal to be able to see a statue; the texts say they don't see them at all. Therefore, it is amazing that we have the karma to see holy objects. We are extremely fortunate because it gives us an incredible opportunity to accumulate merit. You should use every holy object that you lay eyes on, for example, all the pictures of deities in your room, to accumulate merit. That's the reason they exist.

Think of all the stupas, temples and statues in Bodhgaya. Hundreds and hundreds of Indians come to Bodhgaya from all over the country to offer just a few coins to the Buddha statue in the main stupa. Even though their offering is small, because of the power of the holy object, each offering becomes the cause of enlightenment. This is one of the Buddha's many skillful ways of guiding sentient beings according to their karma.

Another ten benefits of prostrations are mentioned:

1. You will achieve a perfect golden body like Guru Shakyamuni Buddha.
2. You will be extremely beautiful.
3. You will have an enchanting voice.
4. Without fear or shyness, you will be at ease among holy beings and other people.
5. You will make devas and human beings happy.
6. You will become magnificent in appearance.
7. You will be able to be with Guru Shakyamuni Buddha and his disciples, the bodhisattvas and arhats.
8. You will have great wealth.
9. You will be reborn in the higher realms.
10. You will quickly achieve enlightenment.

When doing full-length prostrations, which accords with the tradition of the great pandit-yogi, Naropa, you should get up quickly and not stay down on the floor very long. In some traditions, the palms of the hands are held upwards in the prostration. However, the main point of prostrations is not so much their form but that they are done respectfully. Doing prostrations disrespectfully creates negative karma. If you understand this point, you will not be confused by the different styles of prostration. Also, the way you do prostrations is more important than the number you do. It is the same with mandala offerings; it is better to offer a mandala well than to offer it quickly. If you do just one prostration properly, you accumulate unbelievable merit.

If you want to accumulate as much merit as possible by doing prostrations, there are two important points to remember. The first is to visualize as many bodies as possible—either in human form or in the form of a deity—prostrating with you. Also, as you prostrate to the stupa or altar, think that your body covers the entire earth in all directions. The lam-rim teachings say that even if you cannot do physical prostrations because there is something wrong with your limbs or you don't even have any, if you simply visualize your body doing prostrations, you receive the same merit as if you had actually done them.

Therefore, by visualizing as many bodies as you can, you gain unbelievable merit, creating the cause to be born many times as a wheel-turning king. In his lam-rim teachings, Pabongka Dechen Nyingpo said that to be born as a wheel-turning king even once, you have to accumulate inconceivable merit. The *Lankavatara* and other sutras mention that you take rebirth as a wheel-turning king as many times as the number of atoms your prostrating body covers from the surface of the earth through to the other side. Of course, it's not that the only result of doing prostrations is repeated rebirth as a wheel-turning king; the Buddha only mentioned this result to give us an idea of the inconceivable merit we create by doing even one prostration. However, you cover innumerable atoms between one side of the earth and the other when you prostrate, and one prostration creates the cause for that number of rebirths as a wheel-turning king.

His Holiness Serkong Rinpoche once said that His Holiness the Dalai Lama is a wheel-turning king, but I'm not sure if all wheel-turning kings are bodhisattvas. With the power and wealth of a wheel-turning king, you can engage in many Dharma activities and benefit others immensely.

The merit we accumulate by doing one prostration is beyond our conception. The result—all the temporal and ultimate happiness up to enlightenment—is beyond the grasp of our mind. Furthermore, remember that karma is expandable. From one small virtuous action, you can experience many happy results for many hundreds of lifetimes, just as from one small non-virtuous action you can experience many different suffering results both in one life and for many lifetimes. But if you cannot comprehend the cause, there is no way you can comprehend the result.

The second important point is to remember that whenever you see a holy object such as a thangka, stupa, statue or scripture, you must see it as your guru. Do not miss this point. If there is an altar in your house, think that all the buddha pictures on your altar are your guru. In terms of creating merit, your guru is the highest, most powerful object. You get the most merit from prostrating to your guru. Therefore, when you prostrate to holy objects on your altar or elsewhere with the concentration that they are your guru, you create the most extensive merit; much greater merit than you do by prostrating without this awareness.

In a way, you should have a business-like approach to your Dharma practice. Business people try to earn the greatest profit in the shortest period of time. You should practice Dharma with this efficiency. Every time you prostrate or make offerings to holy objects, the essential thing to remember is that they are your guru. With this awareness, what you do becomes most profitable, accumulates the most extensive merit. Your guru, all buddhas and bodhisattvas, all holy objects, are there on your altar. Thinking that your altar holds the essence of all the holy objects of the ten directions, prostrate. Then prostrate to all the holy beings, the buddhas and bodhisattvas, of the ten directions. Then prostrate to all the holy objects—statues, stupas and scriptures—in Tibet, India and Nepal. Using your mind in this way, you create much more merit from basically the same action. This is the wise way of doing prostrations.

After prostrating, dedicate the merit to all sentient beings in the six realms and the intermediate state. Think first of the narak beings, then the pretas, then the animals and so forth, dedicating consciously to the sentient beings of each realm, your merit becoming everything they need to alleviate their suffering and all realizations of the path up to enlightenment.

Sometimes you can combine your prostrations with meditation on guru devotion, thinking that your guru is buddha. At other times, recall the kindness of sentient beings and how much they are suffering. In this way, you combine prostrations with lam-rim meditation, which can inspire you to practice more and more. Otherwise, after you've been prostrating for a while, you might start to feel exhausted and discouraged, thinking, "What on earth am I doing here? Am I wasting my time?" Reflecting on the lam-rim can prevent this from happening.

No matter what vows you might have broken—tantric root vows or pratimoksha or bodhisattva vows—no matter what negative karma you have created, everything can be purified. Out of his incomparable kindness, Guru Shakyamuni Buddha revealed different purification methods, such as prostrations to the Thirty-five Buddhas, who are all manifestations of Guru Shakyamuni Buddha, and recitation of their names. As I mentioned before, recitation of each buddha's name purifies thousands of eons of negative karma. Also, due to the prayers made by these buddhas when they were following the path, each one purifies a specific negative karma.

One of the Thirty-five Buddhas purifies wrong rejoicing, which is feeling happy when somebody harms your enemy or some other person you don't like, or when your enemy gets into trouble or something bad happens to him. It is also wrong to rejoice when other beings create negative karma. Depending on what it is that you rejoice about, wrong rejoicing can create very heavy negative karma. For example, if a Tibetan hears that a million communist Chinese have been killed in battle and, out of hatred, feels happy and rejoices, he creates incredible negative karma. Even though he hasn't been involved in the fighting himself, even though he might have been just sitting on a meditation cushion in his shrine room, by practicing wrong rejoicing, he creates the extremely heavy karma of having killed a million people himself. If you haven't received many teachings and don't know the details of how non-virtuous actions are created, you are in danger of creating very heavy karma.

You don't hear of Lama Tsong Khapa's doing many prostrations to Vajrasattva, but his life story talks a great deal about his practice of prostrations to the Thirty-five Buddhas. Lama Tsong Khapa did 100,000 prostrations to each of the Thirty-five Buddhas. Each day before going to bed he would recite *The Bodhisattva's Confession of Moral Downfalls* thirty-five times. This practice makes your mind very comfortable. In one of his lam-rim teachings, Kachen Yeshe Gyaltsen said that a full monk (*ge-long*) can remain very pure if he practices in this way.

I asked one of my gurus, Denma Lochö Rinpoche, why Lama Tsong Khapa practiced prostrations to the Thirty-five Buddhas rather than to Vajrasattva [see *Teachings from the Vajrasattva Retreat*, pp. 81-82]. Rinpoche replied that with one proper recitation of *The Confession of Downfalls*—which means with correct application of the four powers and meditation on the meaning of the prayer—even the five uninterrupted negative karmas can be purified.

These five heavy karmas—killing your father, your mother or an arhat, causing, with harmful intent, blood to flow from a buddha and causing disunity among the sangha—are called uninterrupted because if you create them, immediately after death you are reborn in the hell realm. Other negative karmas do not necessarily cause you to go to hell immediately; there may be the interruption of some other karmic result before that one. But if you have created one of these five particularly heavy karmas, as soon as you die you get reborn in hell. These are not just heavy negative karmas, but *uninterrupted* heavy negative karmas. However, even these can be purified by practicing *The Confession of Downfalls* just once. This was the special reason for Lama Tsong Khapa's doing this practice. If for some reason you cannot do prostrations, it is still good to at least recite the name of each of the thirty-five buddhas every day, like he did.

No matter how heavy the negative karma we have accumulated, the Buddha has revealed a method to purify it. Through his kindness, we have many opportunities to practice purification. Buddha is more to us than a father. Children trust their fathers with their lives. Whatever happens, children's lives are completely in the hands of their fathers; they totally rely on their fathers. Similarly, we can entrust our entire life to the Buddha. He has shown us that the way to eliminate all suffering is to eradicate the true cause of suffering, the two obscurations, and has taught us the methods for doing so, leading us to temporal and ultimate happiness. The Buddha guides us from happiness to happiness, up to the peerless happiness of full enlightenment. For us sentient beings, the Buddha is our only refuge.

Colophon

Compiled from various teachings by Lama Zopa Rinpoche, including material for a full-length book version of this booklet and *Teachings from the Vajrasattva Retreat. "The Bodhisattva's Confession of Moral Downfalls:*

The Sutra of the Three Heaps" (Tib. *Dung-shag*), translated by Lama Zopa Rinpoche, is from *Essential Buddhist Prayers: An FPMT Prayer Book.* The part about prostrations in general comes from Rinpoche's 1990 Bodhgaya teachings and was originally edited by Ven. Ailsa Cameron and revised for this booklet by Nicholas Ribush.

REFERENCES

Geshe Rabten & Geshe Ngawang Dhargyey, Brian Beresford (tr.). *Advice From a Spiritual Friend.* Boston: Wisdom Publications, 1996 edition.

Lama Zopa Rinpoche, *Daily Purification: A Short Vajrasattva Practice.* Boston: Lama Yeshe Wisdom Archive, 2001.

Constance Miller (ed.), *Essential Buddhist Prayers: An FPMT Prayer Book, Vol. 1.* Taos: FPMT Education Department, revised edition, 2001.

Geshe Jampa Gyatso, *Everlasting Rain of Nectar.* Boston: Wisdom Publications, 1996.

Four

Dedication

Because of the infinite merit of this practice, may whatever suffering sentient beings experience ripen on me, right now. May whatever happiness and virtue I have accumulated—any realizations of the path up to the highest enlightenment—ripen on each hell being, each preta, each animal, each human, each asura, each sura and each intermediate state being.

I rejoice at the infinite merit accumulated by this dedication.

May the precious, sublime mind of enlightenment, source of my own and all other sentient beings' happiness and success, that has not yet arisen in my mind, arise without a moment's delay, and may that which has already arisen increase forever without degeneration.

Because of the merit of the three times accumulated by myself, buddhas, bodhisattvas and all other sentient beings, which are empty from their own side, may the I, which is empty from its own side, attain enlightenment, which is empty from its own side, and lead all sentient beings, who are empty from their own side, to that enlightenment, which is empty from its own side, by myself alone, who is empty from its own side.

Whatever white virtue I have thus created,
I dedicate to be able to uphold the holy Dharma of scripture and
  insight
And to fulfill without exception, the prayers and deeds
Of the buddhas and the bodhisattvas of the three times.

Through the power of this merit
May I never be parted in any future life from the four spheres of
  the Mahayana,
And reach the end of my journey along the paths of
Renunciation, bodhicitta, right view and the two stages.

SPECIAL MANTRAS TO INCREASE THE MERIT 100,000 TIMES

CHOM DÄN DÄ DE ZHIN SHEG PA DRA CHOM PA YANG DAG PAR DZOG
PÄ SANG GYÄ NANG PA NANG DZE Ö KYI GYÄL PO LA CHAG TSÄL LO
(3x)

JANG CHUB SEM PA SEM PA CHEN PO KUN TU ZANG PO LA CHAG
TSÄL LO (3x)

TAYATHA OM PENTSA DRIWA AWA BODHI NE SOHA (7x)

OM DURU DURU ZAYA MUKHE SOHA (7x)

SPECIAL MANTRA SO THAT PRAYERS MADE COME TO PASS

CHOM DÄN DÄ DE ZHIN SHEG PA DRA CHOM PA YANG DAG PAR DZOG PÄ SANG GYÄ NGO WA DANG MÖN LAM TAM CHÄ RAB TU DU PÄ GYÄL PO LA CHAG TSÄL LO (3x)

Due to the power of the blessings of the eminent buddhas and bodhisattvas, infallible dependent arising and my pure, special attitude, may all my pure prayers be accomplished immediately.

With Lama Tsong Khapa as our direct guru in all future lifetimes, may I, my family and all other sentient beings never be separated from the complete pure path praised by all victorious ones for even a second.

Due to the merits of myself and others, may the victorious teachings of Lama Tsong Khapa, Losang Dragpa, flourish for a long time. May all the centers and projects of the FPMT immediately receive all the conditions necessary to preserve and spread these teachings. May all obstacles be pacified and may the FPMT organization in general and the meditation centers in particular—all our activities to preserve and spread the Dharma, particularly Lama Tsong Khapa's teachings—cause these teachings to continue without degeneration and to spread in the minds of all sentient beings. May those who have sacrificed their lives to benefit others through this organization have long, healthy lives, may all their activities please the virtuous friend, and in all their lives, may they always be guided by perfectly qualified Mahayana virtuous friends. May all their wishes succeed immediately, in accordance with the holy Dharma.

Note

For other and more extensive dedications with commentary, see Lama Zopa Rinpoche's *Teachings from the Vajrasattva Retreat.* Boston: Lama Yeshe Wisdom Archive, 2000. Also refer to Lama Zopa Rinpoche's *A Daily Meditation Practice.* Boston: Wisdom Publications, 1997.

APPENDICES

Appendix 1

Practicing Guru Devotion with the Nine Attitudes

"I am requesting the kind lord root guru,
Who is more extraordinary than all the buddhas—
Please bless me to be able to devote myself to the qualified
   lord guru
With great respect, in all my future lifetimes.

"By realizing that the root of happiness and goodness
Is correctly devoting myself to the kind lord guru,
Who is the foundation of all good qualities,
I shall devote myself to him with great respect,
Not forsaking him even at the cost of my life."

Thinking of the importance of the qualified guru,
allow yourself to enter under his control.

1. Be like an obedient son—
Act exactly in accordance with the guru's advice.

2. Even when maras, evil friends and the like
Try to split you from the guru,

Be like a vajra—
Inseparable forever.

3. Whenever the guru gives you work,
No matter how heavy the burden,
Be like the earth—
Bear it all.

4. When devoting yourself to the guru,
Whatever suffering occurs (hardship or problems),
Be like a mountain—
Immovable (your mind should not be upset or discouraged).

5. Even if you are given all the difficult tasks,
Be like the servant of a king—
Perform them with an undisturbed mind.

6. Abandon pride.
Be like a sweeper—
Hold yourself lower than the guru.

7. No matter how difficult or heavy the burden,
Be like a rope—
Hold the guru's work with joy.

8. Even when the guru criticizes, provokes or ignores you,
Be like a faithful dog—

Never respond with anger.

9. Be like a boat—
Never be upset to come or go for the guru
At any time.

"O glorious and precious root guru,
Please bless me to be able to practice in this way.
From now on, in all my future lifetimes,
May I be able to devote myself to the guru like this."

If you recite these words aloud and reflect on their meaning in your mind, you will have the good fortune of being able to devote yourself correctly to the precious guru from life to life, in all your future lifetimes.

If you offer service and respect and make offerings to the precious guru with these nine attitudes in mind, even if you do not practice intentionally, you will develop many good qualities, collect extensive merit and quickly achieve full enlightenment.

Note

The words in parentheses are not to be read aloud. They are added to clarify the text and should be kept in mind but not recited.

Colophon

Written by the highly attained lama, Shabkar Tsogdrug Rangdrol. Translated by Lama Zopa Rinpoche at Aptos, California, in February, 1999. Edited by Lama Yeshe Wisdom Archive Editing Group at Land of Medicine Buddha, March, 1999. The editors are responsible for any errors.

Appendix 2

More Thought Training Meditations

With every action that you do, generate bodhicitta, as shown in the following examples.

When *entering a temple or a room*, pray, "May all mother sentient beings be led into the cities of Liberation and Great Liberation." With bodhicitta, think, "As I enter this place, I am leading them there."

When *leaving temples or rooms*, think, with bodhicitta, "May all sentient beings be freed from the prison of samsara. As I leave this place, I am leading them out."

When *opening a door*, think, "May all the heavy-birth beings be freed from the hell realms by the transcendent wisdom gone beyond. As I open this door, I am freeing them all."

When *closing a door*, think, "May all doors to the lower realms be shut forever and may no sentient being ever go there again. As I close this door, I am sealing all doors to suffering rebirths."

When *bathing* yourself, think, "May the stains of all sentient beings' delusions be completely purified. As I wash myself, I am washing away their stains."

When *sweeping*, think, "May the dirt of all sentient beings' greed, ignorance and hatred be completely purified. As I sweep away this dirt, I am eradicating their three poisons."

When *sitting down*, think, "May all sentient beings reach enlightenment."

When *sitting cross-legged*, think, "May I lead all sentient beings to enlightenment, which is adorned with four vajra postures."

When *getting up from sitting cross-legged*, think, "May all sentient beings realize impermanence and death and the transient nature of all causal phenomena."

When *sitting on a cushion or a bed*, think, "May all sentient beings understand all the teachings of the Buddha in the path of the square (that is, that all the teachings comprise a graded practice that any individual can follow to enlightenment)."

When *prostrating*, visualize that all other sentient beings appear in human form and that you are leading them all in prostrations, while thinking, "May all mother sentient beings be purified."

When *lying down to sleep*, recline in the lion position that Guru Shakyamuni Buddha assumed when he passed away, and think,

"May I lead all sentient beings to nirvana and enlightenment. As I lie down like this, I am leading them to nirvana and enlightenment."

When *getting up in the morning*, think, "May all sentient beings be free of all delusions. As I arise, I am freeing them all from samsara."

When *leaving to go somewhere*, think, "May all sentient beings follow the Mahayana path. As I leave to go, I am leading them along it."

When *reading a book*, think, "May all mother sentient beings realize without confusion the meaning of every word of the Buddha's profound and extensive teachings. As I read and understand this book, all sentient beings are realizing the teachings in their entirety."

When *writing*, think, "May all sentient beings, in all their lifetimes, achieve great wisdom, understand even the most subtle points of avoidance and practice, and realize the two truths. As I write, all sentient beings are accomplishing all this."

When *helping other people*, think, "May all sentient beings be like Avalokiteshvara, who has completed all the holy deeds of a buddha and delightedly takes on the work of others. May I stop the egotistic thought of wanting to progress simply for my own benefit, and never again be lazy or discouraged in the practice of bodhicitta."

When *putting your heel to the ground*, think, "May all sentient beings attain the stage beyond struggle, completely free of all delusions."

When *putting cushions on the floor*, think, "May all sentient beings achieve the method and wisdom of the path to enlightenment."

When *doing up a belt*, think, "May the mental continua of all sentient beings be purified and protected, and through being bound by the three higher trainings, may all sentient beings achieve the two realizations of tantra."

When *going to a quiet place*, think, "May all sentient beings completely avoid all negative actions by completely avoiding greed, ignorance and hatred."

When *offering scented flowers to holy objects*, think, "May all sentient beings complete the practice of morality, thereby purifying all their broken precepts, and may they complete the path of the six perfections."

When *switching on a light or lighting a lamp*, think, "May I switch on all sentient beings' light of wisdom and illuminate their darkness of ignorance, enabling them to see the ultimate truth, through first having lit the lamp of wisdom within myself."

When *eating*, think, "May I see the suffering of all present and future sentient beings and feel their hunger and thirst. May all enjoy the undiluted blissful nectar of transcendent wisdom."

When *taking medicine*, think, "May I become the Buddha of Medicine, who pacifies all pain and whose name, when simply mentioned, alleviates the physical and mental illness that disturbs the practice of the path to enlightenment every day of our lives, and release all sentient beings from every illness." (Before taking the medicine, recite the Chenrezig mantra, OM MANI PADME HUM, the Medicine Buddha mantra, TAYATHA OM BEKANDZE BEKANDZE MAHABEKANDZE RANDZA SAMUDGATE SOHA, or any other specific healing mantra that you know. Then blow on the medicine and, with strong prayers, take it. It is very important to have faith that taking medicine in this way can purify the negative karma that is causing the disease you are treating.)

When *looking at statues of the Buddha*, think, "May all sentient beings receive the infinite good qualities of the Buddha's supreme body, speech and mind."

When *looking at stupas*, think, "May all sentient beings attain the Buddha's omniscient mind, which this stupa symbolizes."

When *talking about or discussing the Dharma*, think, "May all sentient beings understand every word of the bodhicitta teachings and extinguish each and every doubting and unrealized mind the moment it arises."

When *going to the toilet*, think, "May all sentient beings' delusions and mental defilements vanish. As I excrete, I am eliminating them completely."

When *looking at scenery, think*, "May all sentient beings attain the omniscient mind, fully realizing the vast number of varied existences in their absolute pure nature."

Colophon

Translated from Lobsang Yeshe Gyältsen's *Lojong Gönkhyen* by Lama Zopa Rinpoche.

THE ACTUAL PRACTICE OF THE BODHISATTVA'S CONFESSION OF MORAL DOWNFALLS

Begin by visualizing the 35 Confession Buddhas in space in front of you. Think of all the negative karma you have created in this and in all previous lives and generate the four opponent powers in your mind. To increase the benefit of each prostration, first prostrate three times while reciting with each prostration:

OM NAMO MANJUSHRIYE NAMAH SUSHRIYE NAMA UTTAMA SHRIYE SVAHA   (3x)

Continue to prostrate while reciting the names of the buddhas and the confession prayer.

I, (*say your name*) throughout all times, take refuge in the guru;
I take refuge in the Buddha;
I take refuge in the Dharma;
I take refuge in the Sangha.   (3x)

To the founder, bhagavan, tathagata, arhat, perfectly completed
    buddha, glorious conqueror Shakyamuni Buddha, I prostrate.
To Tathagata Thoroughly Destroying with Vajra Essence,
    I prostrate.

To Tathagata Radiant Jewel, I prostrate.

To Tathagata King, Lord of the Nagas, I prostrate.

To Tathagata Army of Heroes, I prostrate.

To Tathagata Delighted Hero, I prostrate.

To Tathagata Jewel Fire, I prostrate.

To Tathagata Jewel Moonlight, I prostrate.

To Tathagata Meaningful to See, I prostrate.

To Tathagata Jewel Moon, I prostrate.

To Tathagata Stainless One, I prostrate.

To Tathagata Bestowed with Courage, I prostrate.

To Tathagata Pure One, I prostrate.

To Tathagata Bestowed with Purity, I prostrate.

To Tathagata Water God, I prostrate.

To Tathagata Deity of the Water God, I prostrate.

To Tathagata Glorious Goodness, I prostrate.

To Tathagata Glorious Sandalwood, I prostrate.

To Tathagata Infinite Splendor, I prostrate.

To Tathagata Glorious Light, I prostrate.

To Tathagata Sorrowless Glory, I prostrate.

To Tathagata Son of Non-craving, I prostrate.

To Tathagata Glorious Flower, I prostrate.

To Tathagata Pure Light Rays Clearly Knowing by Play,
    I prostrate.

To Tathagata Lotus Light Rays Clearly Knowing by Play,
    I prostrate.

To Tathagata Glorious Wealth, I prostrate.

To Tathagata Glorious Mindfulness, I prostrate.

To Tathagata Glorious Name Widely Renowned, I prostrate.

To Tathagata King Holding the Victory Banner of Foremost
Power, I prostrate.

To Tathagata Glorious One Totally Subduing, I prostrate.

To Tathagata Utterly Victorious in Battle, I prostrate.

To Tathagata Glorious Transcendence Through Subduing,
I prostrate.

To Tathagata Glorious Manifestations Illuminating All,
I prostrate.

To Tathagata All-Subduing Jewel Lotus, I prostrate.

To Tathagata, arhat, perfectly completed buddha, King of the
Lord of Mountains Firmly Seated on Jewel and Lotus,
I prostrate.   (3x)

Recite here the names of the seven Medicine Buddhas.

To Bhagavan, Tathagata, arhat, perfectly completed buddha,
Renowned Glorious King of Excellent Signs, I prostrate.

To Bhagavan, Tathagata, arhat, perfectly completed buddha,
King of Melodious Sound, Brilliant Radiance of Skill,
Adorned with Jewels, Moon and Lotus, I prostrate.

To Bhagavan, Tathagata, arhat, perfectly completed buddha,
Stainless Excellent Gold, Illuminating Jewel Who
Accomplishes All Conduct, I prostrate.

To Bhagavan, Tathagata, arhat, perfectly completed buddha,
Glorious Supreme One Free from Sorrow, I prostrate.

To Bhagavan, Tathagata, arhat, perfectly completed buddha,

Melodious Ocean of Proclaimed Dharma, I prostrate.

To Bhagavan, Tathagata, arhat, perfectly completed buddha,
Clearly Knowing by the Play of Supreme Wisdom of an
Ocean of Dharma, I prostrate.

To Bhagavan, Tathagata, arhat, perfectly completed buddha,
Medicine Guru, King of Lapis Lazuli Light, I prostrate.

Finally, recite the confession prayer.

All those [you thirty-five buddhas] and others, as many tathagatas, arhats, perfectly completed buddhas as there are existing, sustaining, and residing in all the world systems of the ten directions; all you buddha-bhagavans, please pay attention to me.

In this life and in all the states of rebirth in which I have circled in samsara throughout beginningless lives, whatever negative actions I have created, made others create, or rejoiced in the creation of; whatever possessions of stupas, possessions of the Sangha, or possessions of the Sangha of the ten directions that I have appropriated, made others appropriate, or rejoiced in the appropriation of; whichever among the five actions of immediate (retribution) I have done, caused to be done, or rejoiced in the doing of; whichever paths of the ten non-virtuous actions I have engaged in, caused others to engage in, or rejoiced in the engaging in: whatever I have created, being obscured by these karmas causes me and sentient beings to be born in the hell realms, in the animal realm, and in the preta realm; in irreligious countries, as barbarians, or as long-life gods; with imperfect faculties, holding wrong views, or not being pleased with Buddha's descent. In the presence of the buddha-bhagavans, who are transcendental wisdom, who are eyes, who are witnesses, who are valid, and who see with omniscient consciousness, I am admitting and confessing all these negativities, I will not conceal them nor hide them, and from now on in the future I will abstain and refrain from committing them again.

All buddha-bhagavans, please pay attention to me. In this life and in all other states of rebirth in which I have circled in samsara throughout beginningless lives, whatever roots of virtue I have created by generosity, even as little as giving just one mouthful of food to a being born in the animal realm; whatever roots of virtue I have created by guarding morality; whatever roots of virtue I have created by following pure conduct; whatever roots of virtue I have created by fully ripening sentient beings; whatever roots of virtue I have created by generating bodhicitta; and whatever roots of virtue I have created by my unsurpassed transcendental wisdom: all these assembled and gathered, combined together, I fully dedicate to the unsurpassed, the unexcelled, that higher than the high, that superior to the superior. Thus, I completely dedicate to the highest, perfectly complete enlightenment.

Just as the previous buddha-bhagavans have fully dedicated, just as the future buddha-bhagavans will fully dedicate, and just as the presently abiding buddha-bhagavans are fully dedicating, like that I too dedicate fully.

I confess all negativities individually. I rejoice in all merits. I urge and implore all buddhas to grant my request: may I receive the highest, most sublime transcendental wisdom.

To the conquerors, the best of humans—those who are living in the present time, those who have lived in the past, and those who will likewise come—to all those who have qualities as vast as an infinite ocean, with hands folded, I approach for refuge.

THE CONCLUSION OF THE PRACTICE

Rather than simply stopping when you have finished reciting and prostrating, remain silent for a little while, generating strong faith that the nectar beams emitted by all the holy objects in the merit field and your recitation of the buddhas' holy names have completely purified you of all defilements, negative karma and downfalls. It is very important to feel very strongly that you have been completely purified and that nothing negative whatsoever is left in your mental continuum. This practice is much more powerful if you conclude by concentrating strongly in this way.

The names of the Thirty-five Buddhas are unbelievably powerful; reciting each one once purifies thousands of eons of negative karma. Remember this from time to time while you are prostrating, but especially when you finish the session. In a commentary to the Vajrasattva practice, Pabongka Dechen Nyingpo mentions that at the end, when Guru Vajrasattva declares that your negative karma has now been purified, it is important to generate strong faith that this is so. The same thing applies in the practice of the Thirty-five Buddhas. The strength of your faith determines how much negative karma you have purified. Your mind creates negative karma and your mind purifies it as well.

DEDICATION

First, meditate on emptiness: "In emptiness, there is no I, creator of negative karma; there is no action of creating negative karma; there is no negative karma created."

With this awareness of emptiness, dedicate the merits: "Due to all the merits collected by having done prostrations, made offerings, confessed, rejoiced, requested the gurus to have stable lives and to turn the Dharma wheel, may I achieve enlightenment in order to enlighten all sentient beings."

Of course, there is a dedication already included within the Thirty-five Buddhas prayer, but you should still make this extra dedication in emptiness at the very end.

LAMA YESHE WISDOM ARCHIVE

The LAMA YESHE WISDOM ARCHIVE (LYWA) is the collected works of Lama Thubten Yeshe and Lama Thubten Zopa Rinpoche. The ARCHIVE was founded in 1996 by Lama Zopa Rinpoche, its spiritual director, to make available in various ways the teachings it contains. Distribution of free booklets of edited teachings is one of the ways.

Lama Yeshe and Lama Zopa Rinpoche began teaching at Kopan Monastery, Nepal, in 1970. Since then, their teachings have been recorded and transcribed. At present the LYWA contains about 6,000 cassette tapes and approximately 40,000 pages of transcribed teachings on computer disk. Many tapes, mostly teachings by Lama Zopa Rinpoche, remain to be transcribed. As Rinpoche continues to teach, the number of tapes in the ARCHIVE increases accordingly. Most of the transcripts have been neither checked nor edited.

Here at the LYWA we are making every effort to organize the transcription of that which has not yet been transcribed, to edit that which has not yet been edited, and generally to do the many other tasks detailed as follows. In all this, we need your help. Please contact us for more information:

LAMA YESHE WISDOM ARCHIVE
PO Box 356, Weston, MA 02493, USA
Telephone (781) 899-9587   Fax (413) 845-9239
info@LamaYeshe.com
www.LamaYeshe.com

THE ARCHIVE TRUST

The work of the LAMA YESHE WISDOM ARCHIVE falls into two categories: archiving and dissemination.

ARCHIVING requires managing the audiotapes of teachings by Lama Yeshe and Lama Zopa Rinpoche that have already been collected, collecting tapes of teachings given but not yet sent to the ARCHIVE, and collecting tapes of Lama Zopa's on-going teachings, talks, advice and so forth as he travels the world for the benefit of all. Tapes are then catalogued and stored safely while being kept accessible for further work.

We organize the transcription of tapes, add the transcripts to the already existent database of teachings, manage this database, have transcripts checked, and make transcripts available to editors or others doing research on or practicing these teachings.

Other archiving activities include working with videotapes and photographs of the Lamas and digitizing ARCHIVE materials.

DISSEMINATION involves making the Lamas' teachings available directly or indirectly through various avenues such as booklets for free distribution, regular books for the trade, lightly edited transcripts, floppy disks, audio- and videotapes, and articles in *Mandala* and other magazines, and on the LYWA Web site, www.LamaYeshe.com. Irrespective of the method we choose, the teachings require a significant amount of work to prepare them for distribution.

This is just a summary of what we do. The ARCHIVE was established with virtually no seed funding and has developed solely through the kindness of many people, some of whom we have mentioned at the front of this booklet.

Our further development similarly depends upon the generosity of those who see the benefit and necessity of this work, and we would be extremely grateful for your help.

THE ARCHIVE TRUST has been established to fund the above

activities and we hereby appeal to you for your kind support. If you would like to make a contribution to help us with any of the above tasks or to sponsor booklets for free distribution, please contact us at our Weston address.

The LAMA YESHE WISDOM ARCHIVE is a 501(c)(3) tax-deductible, non-profit corporation (ID number 04-3374479) dedicated to the welfare of all sentient beings and totally dependent upon your donations for its continued existence.

Thank you so much for your support. You may contribute by mailing a check, bank draft or money order to our Weston address; by mailing or faxing us your credit card number or by phoning it in; or by transferring funds directly to our bank—details below:

Bank information

Name of bank: Fleet
ABA routing number 011000138
Account: LYWA 546-81495
SWIFT address: FNBB US 33

THE FOUNDATION FOR THE PRESERVATION OF THE MAHAYANA TRADITION

The Foundation for the Preservation of the Mahayana Tradition (FPMT) is an international organization of Buddhist meditation study and retreat centers, both urban and rural, monasteries, publishing houses, healing centers and other related activities founded in 1975 by Lama Thubten Yeshe and Lama Thubten Zopa Rinpoche. At present, there are more than 150 FPMT activities in twenty-eight countries worldwide.

The FPMT has been established to facilitate the study and practice of Mahayana Buddhism in general and the Tibetan Gelug tradition, founded in the fifteenth century by the great scholar, yogi and saint, Lama Je Tsong Khapa, in particular.

Every three months, the Foundation publishes a magazine, *Mandala*, from its International Office in the United States of America. To subscribe or view back issues, please go to the *Mandala* Web site, www.mandalamagazine.org, or contact

FPMT
125B La Posta Rd., Taos, NM 87571, USA
Telephone (505) 758-7766 Fax (505) 758-7765
fpmtinfo@fpmt.org
www.fpmt.org

Our Web site also offers teachings by His Holiness the Dalai Lama, Lama Yeshe, Lama Zopa Rinpoche and many other highly respected teachers in the tradition, details about the FPMT's educational programs, a complete listing of FPMT centers all over the world and in your area, and links to FPMT centers on the Web where you will find details of their programs and other interesting Buddhist and Tibetan home pages.

Lama Zopa Rinpoche
Teachings from the Vajrasattva Retreat
Edited by Ailsa Cameron and
Nicholas Ribush

This book is an edited transcript of Rinpoche's teachings during the Vajrasattva retreat at Land of Medicine Buddha, California, February through April, 1999. It contains explanations of the various practices done during the retreat, such as Vajrasattva purification, prostrations to the Thirty-five Buddhas, Lama Chöpa, making light offerings, liberating animals and much, much more. There are also many weekend public lectures covering general topics such as compassion and emptiness. The appendices detail several of the practices taught, for example, the short Vajrasattva sadhana, light offerings, liberating animals and making charity of water to Dzambhala and the pretas.

It is essential reading for all Lama Zopa Rinpoche's students, especially retreat leaders and FPMT center spiritual program coordinators, and serious Dharma students everywhere.

704 pp., detailed table of contents, 7 appendices
6" x 9" paperback
ISBN 1-891868-04-7
US$20 & shipping and handling

Available from the LYWA, Wisdom Publications (Boston), Wisdom Books (London), Mandala Books (Melbourne), Snow Lion Publications (USA) and FPMT centers everywhere. Discount for bookstores. Free for members of the International Mahayana Institute.

OTHER TEACHINGS OF
LAMA YESHE AND LAMA ZOPA RINPOCHE
CURRENTLY AVAILABLE

BOOKS PUBLISHED BY WISDOM PUBLICATIONS

Wisdom Energy, by Lama Yeshe and Lama Zopa Rinpoche
Introduction to Tantra, by Lama Yeshe
Transforming Problems, by Lama Zopa Rinpoche
The Door to Satisfaction, by Lama Zopa Rinpoche
The Tantric Path of Purification, by Lama Yeshe
The Bliss of Inner Fire, by Lama Yeshe
Ultimate Healing, by Lama Zopa Rinpoche

A number of transcripts by Lama Yeshe and Lama Zopa are also available. For more information about these transcripts or the books mentioned above, see the Wisdom Publications Web site (www.wisdompubs.org) or contact them directly at 199 Elm Street, Somerville, MA 02144, USA, or Wisdom distributors such as Snow Lion Publications (USA), Wisdom Books (England), or Mandala Books (Australia).

VIDEOS OF LAMA YESHE
Available in both PAL and NTSC formats.

Introduction to Tantra: 2 tapes, US$40
The Three Principal Aspects of the Path: 2 tapes, US$40
Offering Tsok to Heruka Vajrasattva: 3 tapes, US$50

Shipping and handling extra. Available from LYWA, Mandala Books, Wisdom Books, or Meridian Trust (London). Contact LYWA for more details or see our Web site, www.LamaYeshe.com

What to do with Dharma teachings

The Buddhadharma is the true source of happiness for all sentient beings. Books like this show you how to put the teachings into practice and integrate them into your life, whereby you get the happiness you seek. Therefore, anything containing Dharma teachings or the names of your teachers is more precious than other material objects and should be treated with respect. To avoid creating the karma of not meeting the Dharma again in future lives, please do not put books (or other holy objects) on the floor or underneath other stuff, step over or sit upon them, or use them for mundane purposes such as propping up wobbly tables. They should be kept in a clean, high place, separate from worldly writings, and wrapped in cloth when being carried around. These are but a few considerations.

Should you need to get rid of Dharma materials, they should not be thrown in the rubbish but burned in a special way. Briefly: do not incinerate such materials with other trash, but alone, and as they burn, recite the mantra OM AH HUM. As the smoke rises, visualize that it pervades all of space, carrying the essence of the Dharma to all sentient beings in the six samsaric realms, purifying their minds, alleviating their suffering, and bringing them all happiness, up to and including enlightenment. Some people might find this practice a bit unusual, but it is given according to tradition. Thank you very much.

Dedication

Through the merit created by preparing, reading, thinking about and sharing this book with others, may all teachers of the Dharma live long and healthy lives, may the Dharma spread throughout the infinite reaches of space, and may all sentient beings quickly attain enlightenment.

In whichever realm, country, area or place this book may be, may there be no war, drought, famine, disease, injury, disharmony or unhappiness, may there be only great prosperity, may every thing needed be easily obtained, and may all be guided by only perfectly qualified Dharma teachers, enjoy the happiness of Dharma, have only love and compassion for all beings, and only benefit and never harm each other.

Lama Thubten Zopa Rinpoche

Rinpoche was born in Thami, Nepal, in 1946. At the age of three he was recognized as the reincarnation of the Lawudo Lama, who had lived nearby at Lawudo, within sight of Rinpoche's Thami home. Rinpoche's own description of his early years may be found in his book, *The Door to Satisfaction* (Wisdom Publications). At the age of ten, Rinpoche went to Tibet and studied and meditated at Domo Geshe Rinpoche's monastery near Pagri, until the Chinese occupation of Tibet in 1959 forced him to forsake Tibet for the safety of Bhutan. Rinpoche then went to the Tibetan refugee camp at Buxa Duar, West Bengal, India, where he met Lama Yeshe, who became his closest teacher. The Lamas went to Nepal in 1967, and over the next few years built Kopan and Lawudo Monasteries. In 1971 Lama Zopa Rinpoche gave the first of his famous annual lam-rim retreat courses, which continue at Kopan to this day. In 1974, with Lama Yeshe, Rinpoche began traveling the world to teach and establish centers of Dharma. When Lama Yeshe passed away in 1984, Rinpoche took over as spiritual head of the FPMT, which has continued to flourish under his peerless leadership. More details of Rinpoche's life and work may be found on the FPMT Web site, www.fpmt.org. Rinpoche's other published teachings include *Wisdom Energy* (with Lama Yeshe), *Door to Satisfaction, Ultimate Healing, Transforming Problems,* and a number of transcripts and practice booklets (available from Wisdom Publications).

Dr. Nicholas Ribush, MB, BS, is a graduate of Melbourne University Medical School (1964) who first encountered Buddhism at Kopan Monastery in 1972. Since then he has been a student of Lamas Yeshe and Zopa Rinpoche and a full time worker for the FPMT. He was a monk from 1974 to 1986. He established FPMT archiving and publishing activities at Kopan in 1973, and with Lama Yeshe founded Wisdom Publications in 1975. Between 1981 and 1996 he served variously as Wisdom's director, editorial director and director of development. Over the years he has edited and published many teachings by Lama Yeshe and Lama Zopa Rinpoche, and established and/or directed several other FPMT activities, including the International Mahayana Institute, Tushita Mahayana Meditation Centre, the Enlightened Experience Celebration, Mahayana Publications, Kurukulla Center for Tibetan Buddhist Studies and now the Lama Yeshe Wisdom Archive. He has been a member of the FPMT board of directors since its inception in 1983.